LOOK LIKE THE LEADER YOU ARE

A 7-STEP STYLE STRATEGY FOR AMBITIOUS WOMEN

LIZZIE EDWARDS

PRAISE FOR

LOOK LIKE THE LEADER YOU ARE

"Whether you like it or not, your personal impact and the impression you leave is dictated to large extent by how you look. Rather than leave this to chance, it makes sense to decide how you want to come across, then make it happen. Lizzie is one of the most stylish and beautiful women I know, inside and out. She is no ordinary stylist and Look Like the Leader You Are is no ordinary style book. What makes her really special is her warm, down-to-earth style and no-nonsense approach, and in this fantastic book her practical advice and insider knowledge will help you understand your personal style and bring it to life. Buy it, read it and apply it, you won't regret it!"

Antoinette Dale Henderson, Gravitas Expert & author of
Leading with Gravitas; Unlock the Six Keys to Impact and Influence

"Inspiring, motivating and step-by-step practical, Look Like the Leader You Are is an essential style guide for the ambitious woman who wants to be an authentic leader. I devoured this book, feasting on it's wisdom and soaking up every piece of practical advice. Years of experience as a personal stylist to senior women across many industries make Lizzie the go-to expert on how to look fabulous on the outside, feel incredible on the inside, and glow with confidence all over. I highly recommend it to my clients who want to progress their career and grow their family at the same time. Don't even think about trying to get to the top of your career without it."

Caroline Flanagan, Executive Coach, Founder, Babyproof Your Life & author of
*Baby Proof Your Career - The Secret to Balancing Work
and Family So You Can Enjoy It All*

"*When dress codes have changed and we have such a vast choice of clothing styles to choose from, it is not easy as a woman to know what to wear when we grow in our role as a leader. How can we show up as the powerful leader we are, be taken seriously, without giving up our femininity? Look Like the Leader You Are invites us to take an honest look at who we are; what our body and current choices really look like, how we want to feel and come across to others. It is true deep dive into our personality, to help us become our truest expression through the clothes we wear. It supports us to develop a powerful workwear style that shows the best of who we are, and which supports our goals. A must read for any female leader who is looking to create an authentic professional image.*"

Marloes Halmans, Business and Leadership Coach

"*Look Like the Leader You Are is the perfect complement to our work, to help women move themselves up and out of sticking points that are holding them back. Tackling personal and professional transition, and growth from within, is amplified when we are able to present ourselves as the powerful and effective leaders we are. Lizzie takes a no-nonsense approach to enabling women to unleash their fullest potential through a skilled choice of wardrobe. Her technique is accessible, her advice empowering, and her dedication to advancing other women is inspiring.*"

Lara Holliday, Founder and CEO, Tide Risers

"*Look Like the Leader You Are, is the ultimate practical work style manual. As with everything that Lizzie does, it is imbued with personality, intellect and achievable steps to using what you wear, to benefit what you do. Every working woman needs this book in her life.*"

Alice Olins, Founder, The Step Up Club, and co-author of
Step Up: Confidence, Success and Your Stellar Career in 10 Minutes a Day

"Lizzie Edwards' wonderful book is the missing ingredient in many women's career toolkit. I have bought fifty copies to help all my senior female colleagues look like the great leaders they are, so it is already helping many women go further and faster in their careers, and I can't recommend it highly enough. Indispensable!"

Janet Pope, Chief of Staff, Group Director Inclusion, Diversity & Sustainability, Lloyds Banking Group

"In business, spending time and money on our image usually comes a distant second to the effort we put into our performance. However, the research doesn't lie - success doesn't come from great performance alone. Whether my clients want to 'be taken more seriously', 'feel more confident' or 'get promoted', having been in their (sometimes less than polished) shoes, I inevitably gift them this book. I love how Lizzie acknowledges the judgement and uncomfortable truths, and then, with her expert insights, gives us her practical, easily digestible, step by step approach. At a time when so much can feel out of your control, this book gives you a blueprint to craft your business image with purpose, confidence and individual style."

Gita Trevorrow-Seymour, Executive Coach, Founder, High Definition You

"What you wear sends a powerful signal not only to the world but also to yourself about how you perceive your worth and has a big impact on self-belief. I encourage my clients and audiences to dress to feel fabulous, and to show their body it is respected, appreciated and loved through how they dress. This practical, insightful and easy to implement guide makes dressing to feel confident and fabulous a breeze."

Harriet Waley-Cohen, Speaker & Executive Coach

FOREWORD

The Fold is all about understanding the professional woman's needs in her daily life and creating a stylish, contemporary wardrobe for her. As a workwear brand we wanted to understand how the seemingly simple task of getting dressed impacts your day, your confidence and your perceptions. So, we conducted a joint study with London Business School, surveying more than 1,300 businesswomen across different sectors. The results confirmed what we had suspected; the way you dress can influence your career and your ambitions.

The resounding theme was that first impressions count. 98% of respondents believed their personal style helped them achieve certain objectives at work, and nearly 80% said the right outfit was crucial to boosting credibility in meetings or creating a 'knock-out first impression'.

We are all guilty of judging others based on how they dress, and 74% of businesswomen admitted they assessed an individual's 'executive presence' based on their outfit choices. While more than half of senior businesswomen said 'business formal' was their go-to style, younger respondents had a more casual look, which some felt could be hindering their career progression, 'I've found juniors that dress too informally can struggle to come across seriously,' said one City executive. 'I choose not to take poorly dressed junior colleagues to meetings as I feel they are not good ambassadors.'

When your clothes have the power to influence your career and the way others view you, you need dressing solutions you can rely on to make you feel like the most confident version of yourself. 40% of the women we surveyed felt that getting the 'work look' right was hard: saying they had to 'carefully consider' their workwear, and one in ten described dressing for work as a 'constant struggle'.

Thankfully, stylist Lizzie Edwards, is here to help you navigate the intricacies of 'power dressing' and finding your own signature style in this fantastic book.

Dedicated to creating solutions that you can incorporate into your own wardrobe, *Look Like the Leader You Are* is a fabulous demonstration of practical style advice and shopping tips for ambitious women.

Read this transformative guide and learn the tricks to dressing for success.

Polly McMaster, Founder, The Fold
thefoldlondon.com

CONTENTS

"

VAIN TRIFLES AS THEY SEEM,

CLOTHES HAVE, THEY SAY, MORE

IMPORTANT OFFICES THAN TO MERELY

KEEP US WARM. THEY CHANGE OUR

VIEW OF THE WORLD

AND THE WORLD'S VIEW OF US.

"

Virginia Woolf

INTRODUCTION

Picture the scene. It's a busy weekday morning, you know it's going to be a long day, and you have an important meeting first thing. What should you wear?

Opening your wardrobe, you feel uninspired; so you start rummaging through your unorganised clothes, trying on different outfits, searching for something that ticks the boxes for the day ahead. But you're not sure. Is this dress too casual? Is this top a bit tight? Is this skirt too creased?

Your wardrobe is bursting but you have nothing to wear because your clothes are either old and tired, don't fit, or were bought impulsively and don't work with the other items you have.

Getting dressed is stressful and now you're running late, so you just have to pick something. You regret your choice as soon as you leave the house. You don't feel right and, more importantly, you don't feel confident.

In the meeting, you are not free to perform at your best, either physically, as you fidget with your clothing, or mentally, as brain capacity is taken up with thinking about your outfit.

It should not be this hard, and yet most of my clients had mornings just like this before I took them through my process.

GET READY TO BE JUDGED

For many women, the fact that office style is increasingly 'business casual' and 'smart casual' – giving them the opportunity to reflect their personality in what they wear every day – is not only a minefield but an extra job. It's just another thing to add to the ever-growing list of pressures on working women, a pressure that only increases the higher they rise.

Women are now encouraged into leadership positions in industry, business and politics, and to start companies, go for the top roles, climb the ladder, to 'lean in'.

Businesses are keen to encourage bright, talented women to stay and succeed, but it's not easy for this wave of pioneering women. They have to fight for opportunities, and are judged constantly. And one thing they are judged on (a lot) is what they wear.

Now, I'm sure this won't come as a surprise to you, but a woman's appearance is judged more harshly than any man's. This fact has been proved by numerous studies[1]. So, not only are you fighting against the usual gender stereotypes and barriers, you also have to think much more about what you wear at work than a male colleague in the same position will ever have to. He can pretty much wear the same 'uniform' every day and never have to worry about it. As men have limited options, it's unlikely they will fall into the trap of wearing clothes that could be distracting, deemed overly sexy or inappropriate. But you face that risk with every garment choice, and of course, will be judged for your mistakes.

> "
>
> WE ARE CEOS OF OUR OWN
>
> COMPANIES: ME INC.
>
> TO BE IN BUSINESS TODAY, OUR MOST
>
> IMPORTANT JOB IS TO BE HEAD MARKETER
>
> FOR THE BRAND CALLED YOU.
>
> "
>
> TOM PETERS

This may be an uncomfortable truth, but it is naive to think that intelligence, skill, talent and hard work are all that matter. Believe me, I wish this was true, but in reality, even if you are talented, hardworking, and capable, you can be overlooked if your image does not give the right impression. You may be great at your job, and possess fantastic leadership skills, but if your image fails to make a strong, confident impression, others may doubt your capabilities and promotion, or even your dream role could elude you.

This may be a bitter pill to swallow, but ignoring it, or

perhaps even stubbornly refusing to link your appearance to your success, will not empower you to solve your problem. It shouldn't matter, but it does, and wishing things were different won't change anything, or get you promoted.

Try to think of this positively. If it *is* your image that's holding you back, and stopping you from achieving the success you deserve, then congratulations! This is actually fantastic news, as working on your wardrobe and making changes so you can look like the leader you are, is thankfully a relatively quick and easy process.

HOW I CAN HELP

In 2005, I set up my style and image consultancy to help women to dress well, look good and feel more confident. The majority of clients seek help for their business wardrobes, as they feel their clothes are holding them back from reaching their career aspirations.

I have supported hundreds of brilliant and successful women to look and become even more brilliant and successful. I have worked with female leaders from both the private and public sector across a wide range of industries, including: financial services, banking, advertising, government, media, the law, as well as from large corporations, from Google to Goldman Sachs.

Image matters, and I am passionate about waking women up to their full potential, and showing them just how powerful clothes can be as a tool to increase their confidence and achieve more. I don't try to get a client to look like they have just stepped off a catwalk, but instead, help them to build a wardrobe of clothes they feel comfortable and confident in to create a positive impact at work.

After going through my process, many of my clients have achieved things they had not imagined possible before. They have told me of the doors that opened, and the opportunities that came knocking as a direct result of changing what they wore. They were viewed differently by bosses, given increased responsibility, found the confidence to speak up in meetings, went for promotions, and negotiated pay rises. They attended networking events which they used to avoid because they hadn't been happy with the way they presented themselves, and are now confident speaking at the highest level – in boardrooms and at conferences. They save time by knowing what to wear for business occasions that range from overseas trips to client dinners, and presentations to the board.

TO BECOME MORE SUCCESSFUL,

YOU DON'T HAVE TO CHANGE WHO YOU ARE.

YOU HAVE TO BECOME MORE

OF WHO YOU ARE.

SALLY HOGSHEAD

Essentially, they have been freed of the unnecessary wardrobe stress that was taking up valuable headspace, which is now being put to better use elsewhere.

MY 7 RS PROCESS

This book is in two parts. In Part 1, I explain why and how what you wear matters, to give you an overall perspective, and in Part 2, I take you through my seven-step *7 Rs* process, which I have developed over the years while working one-to-one with women just like you.

This book is your manual, and I will guide you step by step to create a work wardrobe you will love, which saves you time and will give you more confidence to step up to the next level.

The process starts with *Reflect*, where you take stock of who you are, inside and out. It includes activities and questions to help you see yourself from all angles, physically and psychologically, and looks at your goals, qualities, lifestyle, and taste. You'll then *Review* your current wardrobe, to see what you own, and clear out what no longer serves you.

So much of what makes a wardrobe pleasurable, easy to manage and stress free, derives from being able to see what you have, so you'll then *Reorganise* your clothes so that you can effortlessly stay on top of it.

Next, you will *Rethink*, and consider what new items you'll need in your new wardrobe, and the colours and outfit combinations that will make up your own signature style.

Using what you have learned, you will then start to *Research*; firstly, by considering your budget and discovering which brands suit your lifestyle and taste, before looking to see what is available in stores.

You will then be at the stage where you are ready to go shopping to *Replenish* your wardrobe, before finally, I'll encourage you to *Refine* your overall look, suggesting other ways that you can maximise your appearance with optimal grooming: hair, make-up and nails.

Going through my *7 Rs* is a tried and tested way of overhauling your image, and building a wardrobe that works. Throughout the book are *Client Stories*, featuring some inspirational examples of just a few of the women I have taken through this transformational process. These women were just like you, and have gone on to gain self-confidence, career success, and develop real gravitas as a leader.

I know the task may feel overwhelming, and I'm not going to lie, there is a bit of work to do. You will need to put some time aside to complete the activities in Part 2, and I know you are busy.

I want to impress on you that whatever prompted you to pick up this book will not resolve itself without some time and effort on your part, but it really will be worth it. Once you've done it, you'll wonder why it took you so long!

I urge you not to waste any more time; read the rest of this book as soon as you can, and then go back to Part 2 and work through the steps.

PART ONE

1

THE ODDS ARE STACKED AGAINST YOU

I t's not surprising that you find yourself in this predicament. As a working woman, it has never before been more important or more difficult for you to get your business image right. You have less spare time, but there is increased pressure to look good. There is also a greater choice than ever – of styles, fabrics and colours, as well as brands, stores and websites to buy them from. This is overwhelming and creates the perfect storm for confusion. That's without the added pressure of living in an age where image is everything, and everyone seems to look perfect all the time. In this chapter, I will show you how the odds have become stacked against you, so you will realise that you are not alone and there are many, many women facing the same problem every day. The problem is made up of both external and internal factors, which I'll run through below.

EXTERNAL FACTORS

There are certain things that you just cannot escape in today's society, which make it harder than ever to get to grips with your wardrobe. You may not have considered their impact, either individually or collectively.

Dress Codes Have Changed

Business wear has become more casual than ever, and it's increasingly difficult to navigate what is or what isn't appropriate.

Thirty years ago, dress codes were ridged and traditional, but at least everyone knew what was expected and there was little room for error.

Corporate women had to dress like men to reach senior positions, and so wore shoulder-padded power suits to appear more masculine and be taken seriously. The work wardrobe of a female executive mostly consisted of grey or navy below-the-knee skirt suits, usually worn with a white shirt and heels.

In cases when there was one corporate look, it may have been deathly dull, but it was easy. Observe city workers today and frankly, many look a mess. Some appear to have barely woken up, others appear like they are off on holiday, and most look like they haven't even glanced in the mirror. Standards have slipped, but it's not all their fault. With an increasingly relaxed dress code and little guidance, there is confusion, and the risk of getting it wrong. Unfortunately, when you get it wrong, what you wear can negatively impact your career progression.

Brands Have Changed

Fashion retail has changed dramatically over the last decade. There has been huge growth in the number of brands, stores, and new ways that you can shop (with mega malls and the ability to shop from home or office on your computer and phone).

If you have been out of the fashion loop for a while, you can look up from your bubble and not even recognise the stores, brands and styles you once relied on. Austin Reed and many other British womenswear stalwarts have disappeared, so you may find that your go-to store no longer exists.

But as old and trusted brands disappear, new niche brands have appeared in their place. There has been an increase in the number of British 'affordable luxury' and 'direct to customer' online brands, designed specifically for working women, so there are more brands to navigate and familiarise yourself with.

Online Shopping

There has also been an explosion in internet shopping with the growth of huge billion-pound online fashion retailers, such as Net-A-Porter and ASOS, but shopping online is very difficult to get right, and can be a huge waste of time.

For the busy working woman, having shops just a click away should mean you can buy whatever you want whenever you want, but if you don't know *what* you want, it's overwhelming and confusing. Hours spent trawling online stores, without a plan or being clear on exactly what you need, is time wasted, especially if you order items that don't fit or look how you imagined, and need to be returned. This is a common issue, as research shows that almost two-thirds of shoppers who buy women's clothes online have sent something back.

Too Much Choice

When you want or need to buy a new item of clothing, there are an infinite number of options, both online and in stores. It's great to have options, but the amount of choice available of what to buy, who to buy it from, and how to buy it creates more problems.

In *The Paradox of Choice*, Barry Schwartz[2] demonstrates how the explosion in choice in every area of life has become a problem instead of a solution. He writes that too much choice contributes to bad decisions, anxiety, stress and dissatisfaction. When faced with more choice than you need, you are likely to be overwhelmed and confused, and so people tend to avoid taking any action or making a decision. This is certainly true when it comes to clothes, and the explosion of choice has made shopping less of an enjoyable pastime and more of a stressful chore.

Image Obsessed Culture

In magazines, newspapers and on social media, you are bombarded with images of fabulously-dressed women with amazing figures. This creates an unrealistic ideal of the female body, and an unreal benchmark from which to measure yourself. The growth of celebrity culture, social media influencers and bloggers has raised expectations of what women should look like, both on and offline. The 2017 *Status of Mind Report*[3] confirmed that social media sets unrealistic expectations and creates feelings of inadequacy and low self-esteem. Shopping for clothes, or thinking about what to wear when you don't feel you look good enough, makes it harder than it would be if you didn't 'compare and despair'.

The Speed of Life

We are living life in the fast lane and the speed at which our lives change makes it difficult to be on top of your style and keep it aligned with you as you change. One minute, you are at university, without too much to think about, aside from studying and having fun. Suddenly, you're in your first proper job, then maybe you're married with kids, returning from maternity leave, changing careers, moving to a new town or country, and back again! All this seems to happen without you even having the time to look up. So, it can be a shock when you suddenly realise that you are not in your twenties (or thirties) anymore. When you were first employed, you may have enjoyed clothes and had the time and energy to shop, but now you have little free time, you no longer bother to pay much attention to your wardrobe.

And as your life changes, so does your body. Age, children and illness can all have an impact, and dressing your body, which may have been easy at one time, becomes a challenge

CLIENT STORY

LAURA P

C-SUITE EXECUTIVE

CATALYST FOR WARDROBE UPGRADE

A promotion to board level

I am Executive Director of my own company, and a non-executive director on the boards of several other UK high-tech start-ups. I started my working life as a scientist, where the dress code is casual – jeans, trainers, and lab-coat. I moved up to become a project manager, but the dress code remained casual and I became stuck in a rut, wearing the same clothes that I had worn when I was in a lab.

When I was promoted to my company's board, my clothes didn't feel appropriate anymore, but I had no idea how to make a transition in my wardrobe. I was floundering in shops, overwhelmed by trying to work out where to go and what kind of suit to buy, and feeling very uncomfortable every time I tried anything smart on.

I asked various friends to help, but that wasn't successful as none of them were in the role I was in, and they didn't understand the image I needed to project. After the third attempt at trying to smarten up, and a second board meeting still wearing jeans and jumper, I decided it needed a different approach.

Seeing my clothes afresh opened me up to things I had been blind to – items I hadn't realised didn't fit, things that looked old and misshapen, but that I'd been wearing every day. When it was time to go shopping, I tried on things I'd never tried before and gained a new perspective on what suited me, as well as what looked modern and fitted properly. I found that my version of smart didn't need to be a suit after all!

I came away from the process with a new wardrobe that was perfect for my personality and my working environment. The first day I went into the office wearing a new outfit, my boss looked at me, nodded and said, "Much better", which was a great result!

Because I now look like the person I am on the inside, people see me more clearly, and as a result, I now feel in control in board meetings, and more confident in voicing my opinions. I get more respect and people give more deference to my opinions as a result of looking the part, which has led to new opportunities opening up in my career. I can't imagine going back to the image I had before.

INTERNAL FACTORS

Before you try to fix any problem, it's useful to know why it occurred, so that you are aware of the potential hazards and can prevent it from happening in the future. All of the women I work with cite at least one, but often a few, of the following reasons why they struggled with their wardrobe before they took action.

Lack of Time

Most women I know feel there is never enough time, but women with high-powered careers (often along with a family or other commitments), have so many balls to juggle that sometimes the 'clothes' ball gets dropped, and often, they don't even notice.

Maybe you have a furtive glance around the shops in your lunch hour, shop at the last minute, or do it with kids in tow. As a result, you end up with poorly thought out purchases, especially when you don't try things on. Obviously, you can't create a wardrobe of clothes that you look great in and love if you shop like this!

Lack of Confidence

When I talk about a lack of confidence, I am not suggesting you are shy, or racked with self-doubt. You can be successful, outgoing, confident in your work and in many other ways, but not in how you dress. If you catch yourself in the mirror looking older and a bit frumpy, if you find that you have gained weight and everything you own feels too tight, or if your body shape has changed, you can lose confidence.

If you don't feel confident about where to shop or what works for you, it can be overwhelming. You get stuck in a rut, buying the same things that don't work. It's a Catch-22 situation, but once you feel confident about what you want and like, and where to buy it, you'll begin to trust your own judgement. You will be more inclined to try new things, and be braver in your choices. But until you are confident, it's impossible to break out of your current cycle.

Lack of Know-How

Admitting you are out of your depth can be hard. Many women feel embarrassed or think they *should* know how to dress, so don't seek help. But as with most things in life, we are knowledgeable and good at the things we have gained experience in or enjoy doing. If you don't know what to do and do nothing, the problem won't go away – it will only get worse. You may start to underinvest and buy cheap items, as you think you'll probably get it wrong and you don't want to make an expensive mistake. However, this leads to a full wardrobe containing few items that actually suit your needs.

Lack of Interest

Maybe you have never paid much attention to your clothes or how you look, and have never had an interest in fashion. When you got your first 'proper job', you might have dressed in a suit and shirt, or spent years in a uniform, looking pretty much the same every day, not thinking much about it. You looked smart, and that was good enough. As many girls gain their interest in clothes and fashion as teenagers, those who don't are, in my experience, the women who find it harder to navigate their wardrobes in later life. Now you are in a leadership role and considering your professional image more seriously, having little interest in clothes actually begins to matter.

WHERE DOES THIS LEAVE YOU?

The confidence that comes from wearing clothes you love and that show you at your best can be life-changing. Having that kind of wardrobe may seem out of reach to you right now, but it's not. I know it can feel overwhelming when you feel ready to make changes, and don't know where to start. But you have to take the first step, and you have just done that by picking up this book.

If the issues I've raised so far have resonated with you, you'll be relieved to know you're definitely on the right path and this book is going to help you.

And in case you need more encouragement to make the changes, keep reading, as I'm going to talk about why what you wear matters in the next chapter.

2

WHY CLOTHES MATTER

What you wear not only affects how you feel about yourself, how you perform and how you behave, but also affects how other people perceive you. In case you are in any doubt as to why clothes are such an important weapon in your arsenal for career success, this chapter will serve as a reminder. It may also be the additional push you need to give you extra impetus to take charge of your wardrobe.

CLOTHES AFFECT WHAT OTHERS THINK OF YOU

First Impressions

As your appearance is what others see first, the clothes you choose to wear have a huge impact on how you are perceived by others, particularly when you meet people for the first time.

> WHAT YOU WEAR IS HOW YOU PRESENT
> YOURSELF TO THE WORLD, ESPECIALLY TODAY,
> WHEN HUMAN CONTACTS ARE SO QUICK.
> FASHION IS INSTANT LANGUAGE.
>
> **MIUCCIA PRADA**

The concept of 'thin-slicing' is at the core of first impressions. In *Blink: The Power of Thinking Without Thinking*, Malcolm Gladwell[4] discusses how we make an accurate assessment of a person from observing them for just a few seconds, or a 'thin slice' of them. From just a few glances, you decide whether you like another person, whether they're a friend or foe, whether they are like you, how successful they are, etc. If you've ever crossed the road to avoid someone because there was something 'not quite right about them', or crossed a room to talk to someone who 'looked interesting', you've used your ability to thin-slice.

What a woman wears has an impact on the first impression she makes, and her occupational role affects those impressions[5]. Studies have looked into this and found that the more senior the woman's position, the more the outfit influenced how she was judged. A receptionist has a lot of leeway if her skirt is a little shorter than the norm, for example, but a senior manager does not.

First impressions are rarely more important than during a job interview. Your clothes can have a huge influence on the interviewer, whether they know it or not. It's likely that you will be seen before you are heard, and as you walk the five seconds from the door to your seat, the panel will scan you up and down for clues. The impression that you make in those seconds is hard to alter. Before you even utter a word, your image infers a multitude of things about you as an individual – your perceived level of intelligence, competence, affability, self-esteem, confidence, power and success. This is why what you wear is so important. Is this fair? No. But it's happening, whether you like it or not. This then creates the foundation for 'confirmation bias', whereby the interviewer further seeks information that supports their initial judgement and ignores, or gives little importance, to anything that might tell them otherwise.

Ongoing Impressions

You constantly send out silent messages that provide clues to both existing and potential clients and colleagues, who will use them when considering you for a project, job or promotion, or whether to buy your company's products or services. Dressing well and looking like you have made an effort shows others respect, and that you care about yourself.

It's important too that, as an employee, your appearance is not just representative of you, but equally, the organisation you work for, including its philosophy, culture, and standard of service. Therefore, it's important to consider the needs and values of your organisation when considering your wardrobe.

'Dress for the job you want, not the job you have,' is a much-repeated phrase, and it's true for a number of reasons. When those further up in the company can picture you in a more senior role than you currently have, you are easier to promote. Dressing for a higher position than you currently hold enables others to imagine you in the role, and can have a powerful impact on the impression you make. If you look like you can run an important project, lead a team or present to the shareholders, you are more likely to be given the opportunity to do so. You're also more likely to be called on to fill in when your boss or senior colleague isn't available and they need someone to step in. This is why the excuse that 'everyone else dresses down, so it doesn't matter' is a terrible one. Become the person who stands out from the crowd so that when an opportunity arises among those of equal level and skill, it will be offered to you – the best dressed and well-presented employee.

Also, consider the 'halo effect', whereby if someone is well dressed and put-together, we instinctively have greater confidence in their abilities. This is why, for example, if you are in a role where attention to detail is paramount, the wearing of well-fitting, good quality clothes shows both self-awareness and that you do indeed pay attention to detail. If you wish to be seen as forward-thinking and in touch with the times, your look needs to be up to date.

CLOTHES AFFECT HOW YOU FEEL

In my experience of working with hundreds of women, there is no denying that what you wear affects how you feel. When I first talk to a potential client about my services, they usually contact me because of the problems they are experiencing with their wardrobe. However, more often than not, they tell me how their clothes are making them *feel* way before they start talking about how their image may be affecting other people's perceptions.

One of the most common triggers for not feeling good about how you look, and starting not to care about what you wear, is weight gain or an undesired change in body shape. When you gain weight, and are in denial about it and so don't want to acknowledge it, it's easy to start wearing clothes that have 'give' in them, such as jerseys, stretch fabrics, elasticated waists. These clothes, due to their lack of structure, feel sloppy and relaxed but don't make the best of yourself, and often don't support you in feeling good. It's a little bit of a 'chicken and egg' scenario; as a result of a low mood, you don't take care about what you wear or look like, yet not looking your best affects how you feel about yourself.

Your clothes represent your inner motivation and feelings, so it becomes a feedback loop – you feel good, so you'll wear the clothes that make you look good, and on it goes. Research by the University of Hertfordshire into clothing and mood[6] found that 96% of women believe that what you wear affects how confident you feel, and how you feel affects what you wear. They also found that when women are sad or depressed, the three items of clothing they are most likely to wear are baggy tops, jeans and sweatshirts or jumpers. On the other hand, the clothes that made women feel good were usually well-cut, figure enhancing, and made in bright and beautiful fabrics.

Professor Karen Pine, who undertook the research, said, "Clothing doesn't just influence others, it reflects and influences the wearer's mood too. Many of the women in this study felt they could alter their mood by changing what they wore. This demonstrates the psychological power of clothing and how the right choices could influence a person's happiness."

I am not suggesting buying new clothes is the cure for depression or the way to jump-start a new diet, but taking care of yourself, accepting yourself, and wearing clothes that you feel good in, rather than ones that 'will do', affects how you feel about yourself and can impact your life as a result. You may have no desire to wear 'figure enhancing' clothes, or be in a role that requires you to wear structured pieces, such as a suit, but wearing well-fitted, good quality clothes, even when you are 'smart casual', can have an effect of how you feel.

CLOTHES AFFECT HOW YOU ACT AND PERFORM

The clothes you wear can affect your mental and physical performance. Studies have shown that psychological changes occur when we wear certain clothes[7] [8], proving there's a reason why wearing formal office wear and smart, structured clothes puts you in a professional frame of mind. It's not the clothes alone that bring about this shift, but what they represent. It is their symbolic meaning that influences your behaviour. Your brain is wired to match the way you feel with the subconscious associations you have about an item of clothing. When you put on clothing you associate with power, for example, you *feel* powerful, which in turn enables you to *be* powerful.

The clothes you wear can also affect your body language and how you communicate. Take a moment to imagine you are about to go on stage to present to a room full of your peers at a conference. You are wearing a lightweight, pastel coloured sundress and strappy, flat sandals. How do you stand? How do you feel?

Now imagine you are in a structured dress in a dark colour and wearing a jacket and a pair of heeled shoes. Can you feel the difference?

You already know how important first impressions are. If, in those first few seconds of walking on stage, your presence does not command the audience's attention, they may continue chatting. If they start fidgeting as you speak, the energy in the room will be affected. You can 'lose the room' before you even start, and it will affect your confidence, which will affect your delivery, creating a downward spiral.

CLIENT STORY

I was one of a few candidates for a senior role, and feedback from an executive coach was that I should consider my wardrobe and my 'brand'. I needed to show that I could step up into the role, and part of this was more proactively managing my image and my first impression.

I needed to look more 'presidential' but it was important to me that I still looked like 'me'. I am a relaxed and easy-going person, and I found it hard aligning the two parts of me.

Going through Lizzie's process made me take stock, remember what my goals were, and consider the image I wanted to portray. Thinking about my personal style, clothes preferences and what I needed and wanted from my wardrobe helped me see what I was comfortable with or did not want wear, which seems obvious but I had not really thought through it before!

The clear out of all the old and outdated outfits was liberating, and I learned a lot about what worked, and what didn't. It was a letting go of the past and allowed me to start a new chapter.

People noticed an immediate difference and this built my confidence further, and I continue to receive compliments on how I look. I have a wardrobe I love, which I look highly professional in, and have great confidence wearing.

Being organised and a having clothes that work together saves me time, and now, one of my favourite parts of my day is waking up and deciding what to wear. I feel authentically me, but portraying the 'presidential' look I sought. I look sharp, feel sharp, and I am more confident when speaking in large board meetings, knowing that I look the part.

Many professional women underinvest in themselves and dressing their 'brand'. It is amazing how much of a positive change you can make in yourself, and how you are viewed, by investing the time and money in your look. It's well worth it.

SO, WHAT ARE YOUR CLOTHES SAYING ABOUT YOU?

As you can see, the choice you make every morning while standing in front of your wardrobe has an impact on both yourself and others, and can therefore be a career game changer.

If you are someone who has paid little attention to your attire and how you are perceived by others up until now, or given no consideration to the effect that clothes have on how you feel and behave, then hopefully this chapter should have got you thinking otherwise. You'll be relieved to know there is a solution.

3

WHAT'S THE SOLUTION?

By now you have a good understanding of how you dress can impact your career. It can be a tool for advancement or a source of stress, worry and dissatisfaction. Now you are ready to take action.

In this chapter, I'm going to explain why my holistic approach is different to the others you may have come across or even tried already, and it delivers long-term results.

YOUR WARDROBE VS. YOUR GARDEN

This analogy came to me while I was explaining to a client why it was necessary to go through my *7 Rs* Process when she was initially only interested in hiring me to go shopping.

Imagine you have a garden, but plants and flowers hold little interest for you and gardening isn't your hobby. You've not tended it for years, and now it's full of weeds and totally overgrown, so you can't even make out where the paths or beds are. However, you want to start enjoying your garden, make use of the space, and create a beautiful place to spend time. Would you think it was enough to find a flower you liked, throw out a handful of seeds that you've bought and then hope they take root? Would you go to a garden centre, wander around without much thought, buy a couple of plants, and put them in wherever you found a space, and think that would be sufficient? Would you get the garden you desired by putting in such little effort? No, of course not.

To make the best of your garden, you'd first need to spend time clearing the weeds, digging up unwanted plants and taking stock of the garden's situation. You'd then consider your lifestyle and what you'll be using it for, whether you want a BBQ and patio for entertaining, or raised beds to grow your own vegetables. You'd do research, look at other gardens for ideas and inspiration, read books and magazines, and look online at blogs. You'd also get a sense of the style you liked, which might be minimalistic, like a Japanese low maintenance garden, or an English cottage garden with an abundance of flowers and colour. You'd know your budget, get a sense of what things would cost, and invest what was required to get the result you wanted.

As a busy working woman, with little spare time, it's quite likely that after doing this research, you might hire a garden designer to advise and help, and maybe take care of the work required. This would not be embarrassing or thought of as an extravagance, but an obvious solution to save time.

Your wardrobe is way more important than your garden. You use clothes every single day, and what you wear can change your career, and your life. But if you swapped 'garden' with 'wardrobe' in my description, and then considered how the majority of women approach upgrading their wardrobe, you would see that most women don't give much thought to what they need, or do any research. They don't follow a plan, let alone ask for help, and wouldn't even think about hiring a professional. Many feel they should know what to do and how to do it, and believe they should be able to sort it out on their own. This is a recipe for disaster.

If you agree your wardrobe could do with some attention, and your career is important enough to you to take a fresh look at your image, I encourage you to invest both the time and money that is required to do this. The *7 Rs* that follow break down the whole process into manageable steps to get you looking good and feeling great.

WHY YOU NEED A HOLISTIC APPROACH

In the same way that planting a few new plants won't make a garden, addressing only one aspect of your clothes alone is unlikely to lead to long-term wardrobe success. Of course, to start with, you could focus on what suits your body shape, or which colours look good on you, or even book a personal shopper to select some new clothes for you. All of these are useful but only deal with one part of the problem. Working like this, you are likely to run into obstacles. For example, the styles that work best on your body shape, or the colours that suit your personal colouring might not be to your personal taste, be appropriate for work or even available in the shops right now. The instore personal shopper doesn't get to see your current wardrobe or have the time to understand who you are or what your job requires, so they are likely to just kit you out in the latest trends. Ultimately, if you only deal with one part of your clothes in isolation, you won't get a complete or long-term solution.

Even if you have had help with your image to some degree in the past, I am confident you will find the process that follows different, as this time you are going to go back to your foundations and build it up from there.

By working through my *7 Rs* you will gain awareness of yourself, and therefore should you later decide to seek professional assistance for certain steps, or even the whole thing, you will have a clearer idea of what you want to achieve, and gain a better result.

YOU HAVE THE ANSWERS

My process works from the inside out; focussing on you first, and then other factors, such as your business requirements. You won't even start thinking about clothes until you have gained clarity about yourself. You'll think about your qualities, goals and what you want your image to tell people about you. You'll explore what you like and feel drawn to aesthetically, before going through your existing wardrobe, clearing out, and getting organised. You will then find your preferred style, decide what clothes you'll need, and choose a colour palette before you start to research. You'll have a clear plan before finally going shopping. As you can see, each step in my process has an integral part to play in getting you the results you want and deserve.

My experience with clients has taught me that impactful learning happens experientially, in front of the mirror. You will gain the most insights through your own exploration, and by trying things out rather than from reading theory. Throughout my *7 Rs*, I will guide you so that you can see for yourself what you like and what works for you. This will be done by raising your awareness and encouraging you to trust your instincts.

"

STYLE IS PRIMARILY A MATTER OF INSTINCT.

BILL BLASS

"

You may currently find your wardrobe stressful and so not take much enjoyment from clothes or shopping. However, this will change. As you uncover your own personal style and taste, you will find that clothes can become a source of enjoyment and pleasure.

I have some clients who previously had little interest in what they wore, but they now look forward to getting dressed each morning. Suddenly a part of life, seen as purely functional and uninteresting, can become a form of self-expression, creativity and enjoyment.

How much better will the start of your day be when you can open a wardrobe of clothes that you love, which suits and fits you, and is appropriate for whatever you are doing that day?

Now that you have a good understanding of *why* what you wear matters, it's time to jump into Part 2, where you can start to make some changes, and I'll be here to guide you every step of the way.

PART
TWO

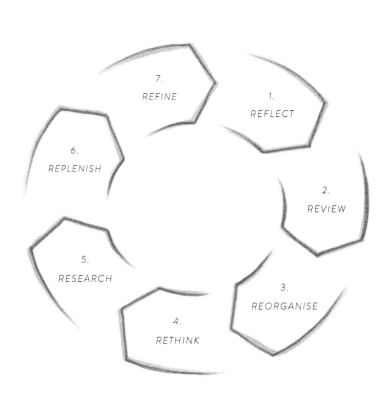

OVERVIEW
OF THE '7 RS'

Imagine opening your wardrobe in the morning and being able to see everything at a glance – clothes you love, that fit, are clean, ready to wear, and where everything is a possible option. Imagine knowing what to wear with what, how to put together the perfect outfit so that you look your best and feel confident. Imagine it taking only a few stress-free minutes, so you can focus on the day ahead.

Sounds great, doesn't it! However, a great wardrobe doesn't just happen, you have to make it happen.

My *7 Rs* process will help you to create a new wardrobe that enables you to project gravitas, feel confident, and look like the leader you are. As you go through these steps, you will gain a new level of awareness. As a result, you'll find it easier to buy clothes that are authentically you and that support your career aspirations. You will enjoy getting dressed, as you will be organised, and know what you have in your wardrobe. When you feel good in what you wear, and receive compliments from others, your confidence will grow. New opportunities are likely to open up, because others will notice that you are beginning to feel more confident.

Throughout the steps, I will give you straightforward direction and advice. I won't be pussyfooting around, as I know you'll want to crack on and get it done. I am here to encourage and guide you through each part of the process, step by step, so you don't need to figure out what to do next or how to go about it.

ARE YOU READY TO INVEST YOUR TIME IN THIS PROCESS?

All my clients go through a variation of this process, and it requires both time and consideration.

It will take you *at least* a few hours to *Review* and *Reorganise* your wardrobe, another few hours to *Research* for a shopping trip, and a minimum of a day's shopping to get you started *Replenishing*. But I'm going to be honest; it is likely to take longer than this, depending on what you want to achieve, how much time you want or need to put in, and how many clothes your wardrobe currently contains.

If you have a lot of clothes, and some women have A LOT, the *Review* step could take a few sessions over a couple of days. However, if your main issue is that your wardrobe lacks many items, you could finish that step in a couple of hours. If you need a lot of new clothes to make your wardrobe work, the *Research* and *Replenish* steps will take more time.

ALL THAT YOU DO,

DO WITH YOUR MIGHT.

THINGS DONE BY HALVES,

ARE NEVER DONE RIGHT.

UNKNOWN AUTHOR

In an ideal world each step would be done in one go, but they don't have to be. You can break the steps down into smaller chunks that you can fit in around your commitments, if that's the only time you can make. Little and often, even 30 minutes a day, or a drawer a day is better than delaying it until you can find a full day.

This is a process not an event, and with consistent effort and momentum, change will happen. Undertake the steps one after the other, without skipping any. To keep the ball rolling, don't leave more than a week between sessions, or it will never get done.

Like almost everything in life, the more you put in to it, the more you'll get out of it, so view the time you'll spend going through this process as an investment in you. Like exercise, you may not like the idea of it, or think you have the time, but once you start, you'll find you actually like it, feel great afterwards, and the results are definitely worth the effort.

HOW TO USE PART 2

Read Through All the 7 Steps First

As you go through the steps, you will be asked to complete activities. Some are questions that will require specific answers, others are prompts that aim to encourage you to think differently and consider things that you may not have thought of before, and a few of them require you to take action.

When you have read through *all* the 7 steps, know what is to come and are ready to commit, get your diary out. This needs planning, so see when you have some time coming up and block this out for the activities, as if they were meetings. Ideally, you will need to be uninterrupted so that you can stay on track and remain focussed.

Make Notes

When answering the questions, I want you to write your answers down, rather than keeping them in your head. This is 'Project Me' and once you get started, you will see a picture emerge. It will be easier to see this, and to remember your answers and thoughts, if you make notes.

You can write the answers and notes in a notebook, or if you prefer to work digitally, open a new note, Word document or create a folder in an app, such as Evernote. Whatever way works for you is fine; the important thing is the information is out of your head.

The notes you make early on will be needed for later steps, so make sure to clearly number all your answers so you can easily refer back to what you have written at a later stage, and when required in the future.

So, let's get started!

STEP 1 – REFLECT

As mentioned before, time passes by so quickly, without you ever stopping to consider who you have become, what is important to you, and what your goals are.

Unless you take some time out for yourself, to remind yourself who you are, what is important to you, and what you want from life, you can lose sight of your goals, and also how you are presenting yourself to the world.

In *Reflect*, you will check in with yourself and your goals. You will take a good look at yourself to notice what you *really* look like; your colour, size and shape, before beginning to tap into your creativity, and discovering what you are drawn to aesthetically –

the styles, shapes and colours – so that you will gain insights into your own personal style preferences.

IF A MAN DOES NOT KNOW

TO WHAT PORT HE IS STEERING,

NO WIND IS FAVOURABLE TO HIM.

SENECA

After you have finished this chapter, you will have an overview of yourself, inside and out. This creates a solid foundation to build the perfect work wardrobe for you.

1.1 YOUR WHY

Take five minutes to think about the following questions in each of the sections below, and write down what comes to mind in your notebook, or wherever you have decided to keep your notes.

I. Your Career Goals

Let's face it, you are not reading this book because you are interested in clothes. Your interest is not about the clothes at all, but what clothes can do for you and your career. You are ambitious, and want to be seen as a leader, and currently, your image is letting you down.

Evidence suggests that being clear on your goal before starting a project means you are more likely to achieve what you set out to do.

So, now you are going to remind yourself exactly *why* what you wear matters to you, and the major reasons you are embarking on this process.

- WHAT IS YOUR ULTIMATE CAREER GOAL?

- WHAT DO YOU WANT TO ACHIEVE BY UPGRADING YOUR IMAGE AND WARDROBE?

- WHY IS THIS IMPORTANT TO YOU?

For example:

- I want to be a CEO

- I want to be promoted to partner

- I want to have more responsibility,
  challenges and an increased salary

II. Your Wardrobe Goals

Think about your wardrobe, shopping and getting dressed for work. What issues and problems in Part 1 resonated with you? Flip back to remind yourself of those now, and answer the following questions.

- WHAT ARE YOU FED UP WITH?

- WHAT IS NOT CURRENTLY WORKING FOR YOU?

- WHAT CHALLENGES HAVE HELD YOU BACK FROM TACKLING YOUR IMAGE UP TO NOW?

For example:

— My clothes no longer fit me since I've gained weight

— My business wardrobe is not leaving others with a positive impression, my clothes are tired and out of date, I waste hours shopping online and send it all back anyway

— I don't know what suits me or where to shop for the style I like

III. The Magic Wand

If I could wave a magic wand, and all these problems disappeared because your wardrobe and clothes worked for you, what would it be like? What do you want it to look and feel like? What is your desired outcome of this process?

Close your eyes. Picture the scene of a weekday morning, with you standing in front of your ideal future wardrobe:

• WHAT DOES THE WARDROBE LOOK LIKE?

- WHAT FEELING DOES OPENING THE DOORS OF YOUR WARDROBE CONJURE UP?

- WHAT DOES GETTING READY FOR WORK FEEL LIKE?

Now picture yourself at work or an important event or meeting, wearing your ideal future outfit:

- HOW DO YOU FEEL?

- HOW DO YOU PERFORM?

For example:

— Now I have my ideal wardrobe, I feel excited to get dressed

— I love my clothes and when I open the wardrobe, everything is in order, ironed and ready to wear; I know what goes with what, and can get dressed easily and effortlessly

— When I stand up to present at the meeting, I feel well put together, and confident in what I'm wearing, as well as what I'm saying

— I am more visible, and therefore speak up more and people take notice of what I'm saying

Personal Branding

It may sound harsh, but in business, you are essentially a commodity. The marketplace you operate in may be global, national or city-wide, and it's likely to be crowded. To stand out and show people what you have to offer, and to reach the top of your profession, you need to consider yourself as a brand.

YOUR BRAND IS WHAT PEOPLE SAY ABOUT YOU
WHEN YOU ARE NOT IN THE ROOM.

JEFF BEZOS

Branding was first introduced in the sixties, for companies that needed to differentiate their products and position them in an overcrowded marketplace. With any product, the packaging sets the expectation for what is on the inside, and tells the consumer what quality they can expect. Your experience of a product, especially the initial impression you get when you buy something new, goes far beyond the product itself, and it begins with how it's presented. The more expensive and high quality it is, the more attention to detail goes into its packaging.

1.2 WHAT ARE YOUR TOP FIVE QUALITIES?

Your appearance is your packaging. It creates perceived value and sets the expectation of your personal brand, telling others what kind of qualities they can expect from you, and what you are about – before you even speak.

KNOW, FIRST, WHO YOU ARE;

AND THEN ADORN YOURSELF ACCORDINGLY.

Epictetus

Below is a list of qualities, many of which are seen as important in business and leadership success.

ACCURATE	ADVENTUROUS	AMBITIOUS	APPROACHABLE
ASSERTIVE	AUTHENTIC	AUTHORITATIVE	AUTONOMOUS
AWARE	BALANCED	BOLD	BRAVE
BRILLIANT	CALM	CHARISMATIC	CHEERFUL
COMMITTED	COMPASSIONATE	COMPETENT	CONFIDENT

CONSCIENTIOUS	CONSISTENT	COURAGEOUS	CREATIVE
CURIOUS	DARING	DECISIVE	DETERMINED
DILIGENT	DISCIPLINED	DYNAMIC	EFFICIENT
ENERGETIC	ENTERPRISING	FAIR	FLEXIBLE
FOCUSSED	FORWARD-THINKING	FRIENDLY	FUN
HONEST	INDEPENDENT	INNOVATIVE	INSIGHTFUL
INSPIRING	INTEGRITY	KIND	KNOWLEDGEABLE
LOGICAL	LOYAL	OPEN	OPEN-MINDED
OPTIMISTIC	ORGANISED	OUTGOING	PASSIONATE
PATIENT	PERCEPTIVE	PERSISTENT	POISED
PRECISE	PROACTIVE	PRODUCTIVE	PROFESSIONAL
RATIONAL	REFINED	RELIABLE	RESOURCEFUL
RESPONSIBLE	RESPONSIVE	SECURE	SELF-CONTROLLED
SELF-RESPECT	SERENE	SOCIABLE	STABLE
SUCCESSFUL	THOROUGH	TRUSTWORTHY	UNIQUE
VISIONARY	WARM		

Now consider the following questions, making a note of the qualities that resonate or come to mind as you go, by using the list above to help you. This is not a definitive list, and there are others that may be more appropriate for you, so feel free to add any that you don't see here.

- What would you want others to know about you, before you have had the chance to speak to them?

- Which words sum you up?

- What words would those who know you well use to describe you?

- What are your key strengths?

- How would you like to be described?

- Is there a quality you're not currently projecting, but would like to?

Look at all the words that you have come up with. Now narrow them down and list your top 5 qualities.

Start each with the words, "I am…"

— I am...

....

Your Current Image

Before we go any further, I want you to assess how much work there is to do, and find out how much your current wardrobe and image reflects you. Are you conveying the qualities you want to project?

Unfortunately, giving feedback on image is a highly sensitive area, even when it is given with the best intentions and to enable the person to develop their career. So you may have never received any feedback yourself.

Luckily, some of my clients were fortunate enough to have had a colleague, executive coach, sponsor or mentor advise them to seek help with their wardrobe, as they felt it was having a negative impact on their career progression. They have unanimously said that although the feedback was hard to hear initially, they are now very grateful it was brought to their attention, and also that they listened and took action.

Some companies and businesses also hire me to help employees with their wardrobes, but unfortunately, this is still a fairly rare occurrence, even though the results are often career changing.

If someone has advised you that the way you currently dress is not serving you, I urge you to view this positively, be glad that someone cares enough to be honest, and take their advice on board. If this is you, congratulations for heeding their advice and making the decision to do something about it by picking up this book.

And if you haven't received any negative feedback about your image, I suspect you feel there is room for improvement.

You are, therefore, going to be your own DIY Image Consultant, and need to be as objective as possible to try to uncover any appearance blind spots you may have, taking a conscious look at your image and rating it on a scale. This will give you a better idea of where you need to pay particular attention.

WE CANNOT CHANGE WHAT WE ARE NOT AWARE OF, AND ONCE WE ARE AWARE, WE CANNOT HELP BUT CHANGE.

SHERYL SANDBERG

You need to know what you look like, top to bottom. So before you start, make sure you have a full-length mirror. And I mean FULL LENGTH, not one that's sort of full length if you lean in at a certain angle. It also needs to be wide enough to see yourself properly, and to be next to or inside your wardrobe, so that it's easily accessible. I had one client who had to go and stand on the closed toilet seat and look at their reflection over a bath! You need a mirror so you can see everything. If you don't have one, I insist you buy one as soon as possible, as you will need it for many of the activities that lie ahead.

1.3 UNDERTAKE AN IMAGE AUDIT

In this activity, you are going to assess three different outfits you currently wear. Don't make any more effort than usual when you're getting dressed, just because you are assessing yourself, as this needs to be an honest exercise. Have your notebook or note app ready, and write down your answers.

- GET READY FOR AN IMAGINARY DAY AT WORK.

- PUT ON AN OUTFIT, TOP TO TOE: SHOES – INCLUDING THE ONES YOU COMMUTE IN, IF THEY ARE DIFFERENT – ANY GARMENTS, LAYERS, ACCESSORIES, AND A COAT AND BAG.

- DO YOUR MAKE-UP AND HAIR AS YOU WOULD, IN THE SAME AMOUNT OF TIME.

- Stand in front of the mirror with your eyes closed at first, then open them and take yourself in for a minute, and remember to view yourself from all sides.

- Take off your coat and change into your 'office shoes', if that is something you do.

The Overall Impression

- Do your clothes look like 'an outfit' – are they considered and well put together, or like individual items worn together with little relation to each other?

- Does your image say what you want to? Does it tell people about who you are, your qualities, your position?

Now you are going to use the following questions and use a scale of 1-5 to rate yourself:

Scale

1   5

1 = Needs improvement, 2 = Could be improved, 3 = OK
4 = Good, 5 = Great

I. Clothes

- SUITABILITY AND APPROPRIATENESS — IS THE OUTFIT APPROPRIATE FOR THE ROLE, YOUR AUDIENCE AND THE DAY AHEAD? IS YOUR SKIRT TOO SHORT OR TOP TOO LOW?

- FIT — IS ANY GARMENT TOO TIGHT OR LOOSE ANYWHERE? IS THE HEM OR CUFF TOO SHORT OR TOO LONG?

- QUALITY — DOES EACH ITEM LOOK GOOD QUALITY?

- CONDITION — ARE THE GARMENTS NEAT, CLEAN, CREASE FREE?

- STYLE — DO THE ITEMS FLATTER YOUR SIZE AND SHAPE? DOES THE STYLE SHOW YOUR PERSONALITY AND LOOK UP TO DATE?

II. Shoes

- SUITABILITY AND APPROPRIATENESS – ARE THE SHOES APPROPRIATE FOR THE OFFICE? ARE THEY TOO CASUAL? OR MAYBE TOO HIGH, AND BETTER SUITED TO A NIGHT OUT THAN WORK, AND THEREFORE A DISTRACTION?

- QUALITY – ARE THEY WELL-MADE AND OF GOOD QUALITY?

- CONDITION – ARE THEY FREE OF SCUFFS? ARE THE HEELS IN GOOD CONDITION?

- STYLE – ARE THEY FLATTERING, COMFORTABLE, AND UP TO DATE?

III. Accessories

Assess the style, quality, and suitability for the following, if you wear them:

- JEWELLERY

- SPECTACLES

- WATCH

- BAG

IV. Grooming

Take an honest look at your grooming to see where there may be room for improvement? Assess the following:

- Hairstyle

- Hair condition

- Skin condition

- Make-up

- Nails

- Teeth

V. Repeat

Change your clothes and shoes twice more so you can make an assessment of three of your current work looks.

What Were Your Scores?

Scoring in this way enables you to see exactly which elements of your image may be letting you down, such as 'appropriateness' or 'quality', and whether these are occurring across different elements of your appearance.

Did you have any 5s? If so, congratulate yourself!

How about any 1s? These are the points to make a priority.

Any 2-3s? These are still important areas that require attention.

Any 4s? These are not urgent, but still consider what is making them less than great.

CLIENT STORY

My image came up as part of my employer's formal annual review process. It was, perhaps, a slightly delicate subject, but the question arose as to whether I 'looked like a potential partner', and unfortunately, the answer was 'No'.

Initially, I was a little affronted, as I naively thought that being good at my job would be enough to get me where I wanted to go. However, I took the feedback on board and HR arranged for me to have support with my image.

Firstly, taking the time to think about my career and life goals made me realise how important getting promoted was. Creating the Inspiration Board was a revelation, as I had thought I wanted to go unnoticed, but realised I now wanted to make a statement and express my personality more through my clothes.

The wardrobe review and reorganisation was really useful, and it became clear I needed to step out of my comfort zone and try something new.

Shopping was another revelation, as I discovered I was wearing the wrong size shoes. This was life changing, as my whole wardrobe had been dictated by wearing flat, lace-up shoes, so I only ever wore trouser suits!

The results have been brilliant. I immediately received compliments from colleagues who would not normally comment, and I moved relatively seamlessly through the promotion process to becoming a partner. A number of people have said that they saw a big change in me, and it was seen as a positive that I took the feedback about my image and successfully acted on it.

Now, I never feel concerned about being appropriately dressed in the office, as I buy things that make me look the part, and I have a wardrobe that I feel comfortable and confident wearing.

The biggest impact has been on my confidence; a total step change. The confidence I now have goes so far beyond the clothes. I sit in meetings as the only woman amongst fifteen men, and know that I absolutely look the part, on a level, and it is very empowering.

I invest more money in clothes now than I could have imagined, but it is an investment in myself and my career that is paying dividends.

Uncover Your Blind Spots

The previous activity may have revealed some areas that you have been blind to, or ignoring. However, being completely objective about yourself is pretty hard, so I would further encourage you to ask one or two other people for honest feedback. This could be friends and family, but it would be more valuable coming from a coach, sponsor, mentor, colleague, or a boss with whom you have a good relationship and whose opinion you value.

It is important that the person giving the feedback is aware of your career aspirations, understands the environment and industry you work in, and the purpose of the exercise. They will need to frame their feedback from that perspective, and be more thoughtful and potentially more critical than they might otherwise be. You must be prepared to take on board their comments without taking it personally, or becoming defensive or sensitive. This is absolutely crucial, as it is possible you may hear something critical, which feels personal and hurts. Please remember how helpful this feedback will be – it can be the first step to you fixing whatever issues come up. You want positive change, and to look like a strong leader.

> " THE UPSIDE OF PAINFUL KNOWLEDGE IS SO
> MUCH GREATER THAN THE DOWNSIDE OF
> BLISSFUL IGNORANCE. "
>
> **SHERYL SANDBERG**

Size and Shape

Size is an area where many women hold on to an out of date or inaccurate mental picture. If you used to be smaller when you were younger, or pre-children, you may still harbour a dream that you can get back there again. It's time to let it go. Acknowledging your present reality allows you to dress in clothes that fit and flatter you, and you will feel better for it.

Clothes that are too small serve as a constant reminder you are bigger than you want to be, or once were. If you are overweight, tight clothes make you look more so, whereas in the correct size, you will look at ease, self-aware and self-assured.

On the other hand, you may be overestimating your size and wear clothes that are too big, that are sloppy and overwhelm you. If you have lost weight and are now smaller than you've been in the past, reality may not have yet caught up and you may be buying a size that doesn't make the best of you.

In this next activity, you are going to get acquainted with yourself physically, so that you have *completely* accurate information, as it's difficult to create a great wardrobe without first being totally honest about what you are working with. If you are prone to self-judgement, I urge you to silence that inner voice. This is also not the time for comparisons of how you used to look, or what size you once were. This is about acknowledging your present-day reality, which you'll need to do so that you can dress yourself as your BEST self, as you are today.

Accepting yourself at the size you currently are will also free up a lot of headspace, to make dressing a lot easier. Remember, your clothing size and body measurements don't mean anything about you, but are a merely a tool to help you select the right size.

1.4 MEASURE UP

In order to get an accurate record of the UK clothing size that fits your body, so you can use it as a guide to convert easily while shopping across different brands, you are going to measure yourself.

First, you'll need to get yourself a tape measure. Make sure this is kept level.

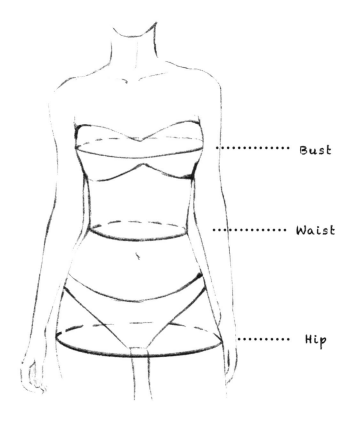

Bust

Waist

Hip

Bust

Measure under your armpits, around your shoulder blades, and over the fullest part of your bust. Don't pull the tape measure too hard.

Waist

Measure around your natural waistline. This is the narrow part of your waist, about an inch above your navel. Relax and breathe out before you measure.

Hip

The hip should be measured around its fullest part (about 8 inches below your waist, approximately crotch level) *not* your hip bone.

Make a note of your bust, waist and hip measurements in both centimetres and inches.

Then, use the chart below, featuring the most common sizes, to check your UK standard clothing size, and make a note of that too.

Size	Bust		Waist		Hips	
	cm	in	cm	in	cm	in
8	81	31.9	61	24.0	89	35.0
10	85	33.5	66	26.0	93	36.6
12	89	35.0	71	28.0	96.5	38.0
14	93	36.6	76	29.9	101.5	40.0
16	97	38.2	81	31.9	106.5	41.9
18	102	40.2	86	33.9	112	44.1

You will be referring back to these measurements in the later steps, when it's time to *Research* and *Replenish*. And in the future, whenever you visit a brand's store or website, look up the measurements they use for their sizing (this can change from brand to brand) to give yourself a much better chance of selecting the correct size the first time.

1.5 MIRROR MIRROR

I. Your Shape

I now want you to get to know the shape of your body.

You may rarely, or never, look at yourself properly in your underwear in the mirror, and therefore, you will have a lack of awareness about what your body actually looks like top to toe, from all sides.

Stand in your underwear in front of the mirror and take some time to look at yourself properly, so you can assess your shape and proportions. Please be kind to yourself and non-judgemental about what you see, and I also encourage you to let go of body shape categories that you may have come across in the past, for example, labelling yourself as a 'pear' or 'apple'.

This quick activity is for awareness, but make notes, as you may want to refer back to them later, particularly before you *Research* and *Replenish*.

As you view yourself, consider the following questions to get you started:

- Do your shoulders slope, or is one higher than the other?

- Are your shoulders narrower than your hips?

- Do you go in at the waist, or are you straight up and down, or are you wider in a certain section?

- Are your legs long in comparison to a shorter torso, or do you have a long torso and shorter legs?

- Is your neck particularly long or short?

- What are your assets to be highlighted?

- Are there areas that you are less than confident about that you would like to camouflage?

- Is your body shape sharper edged and straight lined, softly curved and fleshy, or muscular and taught?

- Would you describe yourself as small, medium or large framed?

- Does anything else stand out?

II. Your Bra

One of the most important factors that enables you to look good in your clothes is your underwear, so while you are in front of the mirror, I now want you to assess the fit of your bra.

- DO YOU THINK YOUR CHEST WOULD SIT HIGHER WITH A BETTER FITTING BRA?

- CHECK THAT THE CENTRAL PART OF YOUR BRA SITS FLAT ON YOUR SKIN, WITHOUT ANY GAPS OR IT DIGGING IN.

Here are some tips on what to look for:

- THE MAIN SUPPORT COMES FROM THE CHEST BAND, THE MOST IMPORTANT PART OF THE BRA. IF THE BACK RIDES UP INTO AN ARC AND DOESN'T SIT HORIZONTALLY, YOU LIKELY NEED TO GO DOWN A CHEST SIZE (THE NUMBER, I.E. 34), AND UP ONE OR TWO CUP SIZES (THE LETTER, B, C, D, ETC.). FOR EXAMPLE, YOU NEED TO WEAR 34D BUT CURRENTLY WEAR 36C. IN MY EXPERIENCE, THIS IS WHERE MOST SIZE MISTAKES OCCUR.

- THE UNDERWIRE SHOULD SIT COMFORTABLY UNDER YOUR BUST. IF IT SITS ON YOUR BREAST OR DIGS IN, THE CUP SIZE IS TOO SMALL FOR YOU, OR IF THERE ARE WRINKLES AROUND THE CUP, IT IS TOO BIG.

- THE BRA STRAPS SHOULD SIT ON YOUR SHOULDERS WITHOUT SLIPPING OFF, DIGGING IN OR LEAVING INDENTATIONS. THE STRAPS ARE THERE TO HELP TO

BALANCE THE WEIGHT OF YOUR BREASTS AND ASSIST THE CHEST STRAP, BUT NOT HOLD YOUR BREASTS UP.

- YOUR BRA SHOULD BE FASTENED ON THE MIDDLE HOOK, PARTICULARLY WHEN IT IS NEW, AS THIS ALLOWS YOU TO GAIN OR LOSE AN INCH, OR FOR ADJUSTMENT AS THE BRA STRETCHES OVER TIME.

III. Your Colouring

The purpose of this exercise is to make you stop for a few minutes and *really* notice your inherent colouring. The questions may sound obvious, but look at your face in the mirror and answer the following questions, noting the answers.

- IS YOUR SKIN LIGHT, MEDIUM, OR DARK?

- WHAT COLOUR IS YOUR HAIR? BLONDE, BROWN, GREY, RED, BLACK? AND NOTE, IS THE SHADE LIGHT, MEDIUM OR DARK?

- WHAT COLOUR ARE YOUR EYES? LOOK CLOSELY AND SEE THE DIFFERENT COLOURS IN THE IRIS. ALSO, NOTE WHETHER YOUR EYES ARE LIGHT, MEDIUM OR DARK?

These colours, found in your inherent colouring, will always suit you, and are worth considering when you come to choose a colour palette.

If you have a mix of light and dark colour values, you have what is known as 'high contrast' colouring, but if you are predominately *either* light, *or* dark, *or* medium, you appear as 'low contrast'.

Style Inspiration and Aspiration

The next stage of your self-reflection is to think about your aesthetic preferences, to begin to uncover and recognise your own personal taste. If you struggle with your style, these exercises will enable you to discover what you really like, which for me, is even more important to be aware of than what colours suit you or what shape and size you are.

Interior designers, graphic designers, fashion designers and architects use 'Inspiration Boards', also known as 'Mood Boards', to inspire, influence and motivate them at the start of a new project. Inspiration comes from surprising places, and the things you like say a lot more about you than you may realise.

I want you to emerge yourself in art, interiors, design, and style. Start to notice what others are wearing and see what resonates with you, as your taste in architecture, furniture – even your favourite painting, flower, car or hotel – all say something about what pleases you aesthetically.

1.6 CREATE AN INSPIRATION BOARD

In order to get clear about your personal image and style, you need to be inspired, and collecting images of what inspires and motivates you is a great way to start clarifying your style aspirations.

Don't just think about fashion, but pull together images of things you love from everywhere.

" YOU CAN FIND INSPIRATION IN EVERYTHING.

IF YOU CAN'T, THEN YOU'RE NOT

LOOKING PROPERLY.

PAUL SMITH

Remember, this is not a shopping list but an *Inspiration Board*, so it's not about finding clothes you would wear, it is about finding images that excite you on a deeper, subconscious level. Go with your instincts. You do not need to know yet why you have chosen the things you have; just enjoy the process of noticing and collecting the images.

- Get a board of A2 size or bigger to display all your pictures. It can be a corkboard and some pins, if you would like to keep updating it going forward, or card and glue, which is more permanent.

- Explore fashion, lifestyle and interior magazines and catalogues. Tear and cut out images of anything you love.

- It may just be the colour, a small element or feature, or it could be the entire image. It may be the style of a dress you would love to own, or more about a feeling you get from the image of it. Don't question why you like something, and if it is clothing, do not think: "I could never wear it" or "I couldn't walk in those shoes."

- Collect images of the places you love: scenery, colours, wallpaper patterns, buildings, art, paintings, your favourite flowers, tiles and interiors.

- Find a picture of a person whose style you admire.

- Go online for specific items, paintings, colours, or to find a picture of something you know you'd love to use on your board.

- Look at lifestyle and fashion blogs.

- When you have a selection of 30-50 images, go through them and take out any that no longer inspire you, or any you have forgotten why you chose.

- Pin or stick them to the board or card, overlapping so they are and totally filling the board, creating a collage of inspirational images.

1.7 DISCOVERING YOUR STYLE WORDS

"

STYLE IS A WAY OF SAYING WHO YOU ARE

WITHOUT HAVING TO SPEAK.

"

RACHEL ZOE

Now you have created your *Inspiration Board*, stand back and look at the whole board as one.

- WHAT STRIKES YOU ABOUT THE COLLECTION OF IMAGES WHEN THEY ARE VIEWED TOGETHER?

- WHAT THEME STANDS OUT? IT COULD BE A COLOUR PALETTE, STYLE OR MAYBE A GENERAL FEELING.

Perhaps it will confirm what you know, but it may reveal a fresh, new direction. For example, you may uncover a love of minimalism – pictures of Scandinavian architecture, a monochrome colour theme and simple clothes – yet your current wardrobe is full of pattern, colours and items with a lot of design details, revealing how your current wardrobe isn't you anymore.

- WRITE DOWN THE IMPRESSION YOU SEE AND WHAT YOU FEEL FROM THE COLLECTION OF IMAGES, ESPECIALLY ANY ADJECTIVES THAT COME TO YOU WHEN VIEWING THE OVERALL IMPRESSION. EXAMPLES OF WORDS THAT MAY COME UP ARE: LUXURIOUS, UNDERSTATED, RELAXED, ELEGANT, MINIMALIST, STRONG, FUN, CHIC, EXPENSIVE, BUT OF COURSE, THERE ARE MANY OTHERS.

- NOW LOOK AT EACH IMAGE YOU CHOSE IN TURN AND ASK YOURSELF THE FOLLOWING QUESTIONS. YOU MAY FIND THAT ANSWERING OUT LOUD HELPS AND THEN WRITING DOWN WHAT COMES UP.

  — Why do I love it?

  — What does it say?

  — How does it make me feel?

- REVIEW THE NOTES YOU HAVE TAKEN. WHICH WORDS COME UP REPEATEDLY? HIGHLIGHT ANY DESCRIPTIVE WORDS. DO ANY OF THEM ESPECIALLY CAPTURE HOW YOU WOULD LIKE TO BE SEEN, OR HOW YOU WANT TO FEEL?

- FINALLY, CHOOSE FIVE WORDS THAT DESCRIBE WHAT YOU WOULD LOVE TO CONVEY THROUGH YOUR CLOTHES.

- THESE FIVE WORDS ARE NOW YOUR *STYLE WORDS*. WRITE THEM LARGE OR PRINT THEM OUT AND ADD THEM ONTO YOUR COLLAGE *INSPIRATION BOARD*.

Congratulations on creating your *Inspiration Board*. It will help you as you go through the steps ahead. Hang it where you will see it as you go through your clothes. It will steer you, and keep you on track when you have decisions to make about what to keep, what to buy and what to wear.

Style Aspiration on Pinterest

Pinterest is a great aspirational tool, allowing you to search and collate images. Think of it like digitally pinning a picture on a board, like you did in the previous activity. It can be used to search for images by using terms such as 'smart casual workwear' and 'office dresses' for pictures of stylish women you admire, or looks you would like to wear in real life, such as 'French chic' or 'effortless workwear'.

> **"**
>
> ALWAYS KEEP YOUR EYES OPEN.
> KEEP WATCHING. BECAUSE WHATEVER YOU
> SEE CAN INSPIRE YOU.
>
> **"**
>
> GRACE CODDINGTON

If you are not particularly into clothes, being aware of the current 'look' is helpful, and by using Pinterest, you'll begin to get a feel for it. Everything will look and feel familiar when you get to the *Research* phase, and your shopping trip.

1.8 CREATE ASPIRATIONAL STYLE BOARDS ON PINTEREST

- If you haven't used it before, from your computer, set up an account at www.pinterest.com. In the 'Help Centre', there are clear instructions to help you get started. The best way to learn is by having a go, and it will soon begin to make sense.

- To start, create 5-10 separate boards for your main wardrobe and style categories, such as 'office style', 'work dresses', 'weekend looks', 'coats', 'statement necklaces', women I admire' or 'colours I like'. You can add new boards as you go and move the images around.

- Undertake searches for 'pins'. To find images, use terms such as 'workwear', 'work dresses', 'smart casual looks', and you can also search for specific women – both real and fictional – that you have admired. TV shows can offer great workwear inspiration. For example, 'Good Wife Alicia style' or 'Clare Underwood wardrobe'. You can also search for well-known female business leaders or celebrities who you admire the style of, such as 'Christine Lagarde style' or 'Angelina Jolie style'.

- Pin a minimum of 30 images, but more if you get on a roll.

1.9 MAKE PINTEREST NOTES

Now you have amassed some pins, notice how your choices and style evolve and become more specific.

- Editing is an important part of the process, so distil and hone in on your preferred style. Once you have a large number of Pins, reassess and delete those that no longer inspire you.

- Look through the boards at the outfits you pinned, and look at each image in turn, just as you did in the *Inspiration Board* exercise.

- Write down any words that come to you to describe the outfits, items and women that you have pinned. Do they align with your *Qualities* and *Style Words*? If any come up or particularly resonate, add them to the list of the *Style Words* and onto your board.

- Which garment shapes and overall silhouettes come up most often? Maybe you prefer crew to V-neck. Do you prefer cropped, slim trousers? Do you favour straight, loose fit, shift-style dresses, or those that come in at the waist with a full skirt? Are you drawn to dresses or smart separate combinations?

- Make a note of anything you see about the way any outfits are combined. Are there any accessories you notice that help to pull an outfit together? Or any combinations you wouldn't have considered that work?

STEP 1 RECAP

You should now have:

- SET YOUR 'WHY' – YOUR CAREER AND WARDROBE GOALS

- NOTED YOUR TOP FIVE *QUALITIES*

- CONDUCTED AN IMAGE AUDIT OF THREE WORK OUTFITS

- GAINED IMAGE FEEDBACK FROM ANOTHER PERSON

- UNDERSTOOD YOUR SIZE, SHAPE AND COLOURING

- CREATED AN *INSPIRATION BOARD*

- DISCOVERED YOUR *STYLE WORDS*

- CREATED ASPIRATIONAL STYLE BOARDS ON PINTEREST

- MADE NOTES ON YOUR PINTEREST BOARDS

What you discovered during the activities in this *Reflect* step may have uncovered something unexpected and even been a revelation, or it may have confirmed your instincts and what you already knew. Keep your notes where you can find them, as you will be referring to them in the later steps.

You are now ready to move on to the next step in the process; it's time to *Review* your current wardrobe.

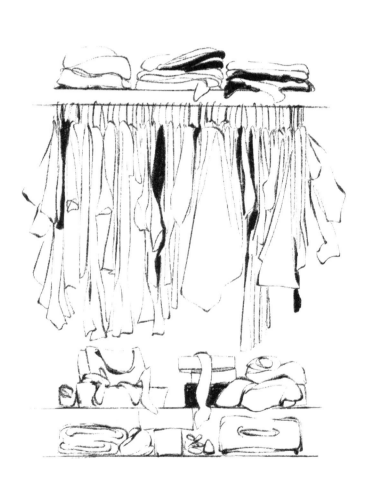

STEP 2 – REVIEW

In the previous step, we looked at *you*. Now we need to turn our attention to your current wardrobe. It's time for a clear out!

Before you start going through your clothes, I want to make sure that you are prepared and in the right headspace, so remember your goals and why you are doing this. Remember, it's not about the clothes, it's about so much more, and believe me, it will be worth it in the end.

The more clothes you own, the more ruthless I want you to be.

I undertake so many wardrobe sessions where a client says they have recently had a clear out, and yet there are still items that don't fit, they don't like, or haven't worn for years. Having items in the wardrobe that you don't wear drains your energy and clutters your brain, serving as a reminder of wasted money, a lifestyle that is no longer yours, or a size you used to be, and an 'overfull wardrobe but nothing to wear' situation. As I constantly have to remind clients, there are only seven days in a week, and you will tend to wear the same clothes most of the time.

Some stylists and declutterers talk about only keeping clothes that you LOVE as a benchmark of what to get rid of. That is worth considering as you review each item, but I feel that is an idealistic goal and too high a bar to set. You may be one of those people who will *never* be that passionate about their clothes, especially as many items you keep will be practical and functional. However, you must at least really like every item you keep, even if it's owned for its practical benefits. If you don't really like it, but need it, make a note so you can get a better replacement.

Remember, the goal at the end of this process is a wardrobe where everything that faces you when you open the doors or pull out a drawer is an option to put on that day. Every item should fit you, be clean, and remain in good condition.

2.1 WARDROBE REVIEW PREPARATION

To make sure you are prepared, do the following:

- It's essential to have a full-length mirror next to the wardrobe, so if you haven't got one there, sort that out now, before you start the next section.

- Make sure you have plenty of large black bin bags, some paper or Post-It notes, and a pen.

- Pull out your notes with your Top Five *Qualities* and *Style Words*. Make sure your *Inspiration Board* is somewhere you can see it, so you can read the words and be reminded of the feeling and aesthetic you are aiming for.

2.2 TAKE IT ALL IN, AND TAKE PICTURES

If you have a lot of clothes and your wardrobe is very messy, this next exercise can feel totally overwhelming, but don't worry – it won't be for long and it will get done. If you feel like this then remember, '*the only way out is through*', and I promise that you will feel fantastic once it's done, as well as excited that you've taken this step now. If you get a sinking feeling, it's probably rising up in you most days when you open the wardrobe anyway, and it's not a good feeling to start the day with, ever. Soon it will feel very different, I promise!

- BEFORE YOU JUMP IN, OPEN YOUR WARDROBE(S) AND HAVE A LOOK AT WHAT IS IN FRONT OF YOU. IF YOU HAVE DRAWERS OR CUPBOARDS IN OTHER ROOMS, OPEN THEM TOO, TO GET A SENSE OF HOW MUCH YOU HAVE.

- TAKE SOME 'BEFORE' PICTURES OF YOUR WARDROBE(S) AND DRAWERS SO THAT YOU CAN SEE THE PROGRESS YOU'VE MADE AND SEE WHAT YOU'VE ACCOMPLISHED WHEN YOU FINISH.

2.3 CLEAR OUT NON-CLOTHING RELATED ITEMS

- BEFORE YOU START ON YOUR CLOTHES, YOU NEED TO DEAL WITH OTHER FORMS OF CLUTTER THAT CAN CREEP INTO A WARDROBE AND CREATE MESS AND DISTRACTION. WARDROBES ARE FOR CLOTHES, SHOES, BAGS AND ACCESSORIES ONLY, NOTHING ELSE. NOT CHRISTMAS PRESENTS, PHOTO ALBUMS, TOYS, FILES OR PAPERWORK. IF THERE IS ANYTHING ELSE IN YOUR WARDROBE, OR CLOTHING DRAWERS, PLEASE FIND A NEW HOME FOR IT NOW.

2.4 CREATE PILES

The clothes that are not going immediately back into your wardrobe will fall in one of the following six categories. Familiarise yourself with these categories, and get six bits of paper or Post-It notes to create a label for each pile. Allocate and create a space for each pile, or have a bin liner ready, to avoid confusion later.

Going

- SELL – FOR DESIGNER OR VINTAGE ITEMS IN GOOD CONDITION. THESE CAN BE SOLD VIA EBAY, A DRESS AGENCY OR A DESIGNER RESALE WEBSITE.

- CHARITY SHOP OR FRIEND – FOR DECENT CLOTHES THAT A FRIEND OR CHARITY SHOP CAN MAKE USE OF.

- RUBBISH/RECYCLING – FOR CLOTHES THAT ARE DAMAGED, STAINED OR WORN OUT.

Staying

- DRY-CLEANING – FOR CLOTHES THAT ARE STAINED, OR COULD DO WITH A PRESS AND REFRESH.

- ALTERATIONS – for clothes in need of taking in, taking up, mending or having missing buttons sewn on.

- 'TIME CAPSULE' STORAGE – for clothes that currently don't fit, but will do within a few months.

What to Let Go Of

As you go through your wardrobe, you may find it hard to let go of items, even though they no longer serve you. To help yourself stay on track, keep referring back to your *Inspiration Board*, *Style Words*, and *Qualities*. Often, just holding an item up against yourself in front of the mirror and asking the question, *"What does this item say about me?"* or *"Does this say —?"* is all you need to ask before it goes straight into a bin liner without a second thought!

As you go through your wardrobe, you will come across the following, and I urge you to get rid of them all without a second thought. There is no place for any of the following items in your upgraded wardrobe:

Uncomfortable

Life is too short to wear uncomfortable clothes.

Get rid of any uncomfortable items, i.e. shoes you can't walk in or that don't fit, dresses that require pulling down, or blouses that need constant adjusting. Innovation in man-made fibres has created amazing fabrics that are tactile and stretch to fit comfortably, so replace any items you have in cheap fabrics that make you sweat or itch. Cut out any itchy labels.

IF YOU'RE NOT COMFORTABLE,

NO MATTER HOW WELL DRESSED YOU ARE,

YOU'RE NOT GOING TO LOOK RIGHT.

I'D RATHER BE HAPPY AND FEEL COMFY.

IRIS APFEL

The *only* exception to keeping an uncomfortable item is if you love it so much, you don't care that it's uncomfortable, and you genuinely wear it anyway, such as a pair of high-heeled shoes.

Dated

If you don't own many clothes, don't shop very often or keep up with what's happening in trends, your image can become dated without you even knowing it. Clothes change, often in subtle, gradual ways that may not be noticeable over a year or two, but five years is a good benchmark to keep in mind, especially when assessing jackets, suits and trousers. The collar of an old suit will date your look, however great the brand or high the quality, so that first 'expensive' suit, or *any* suit you have had over 10 years, is now way past it.

I regularly come across black tie evening dresses, hanging unworn for years. When an occasion arises that warrants a glamorous dress, it is likely to be a special evening. Wearing a dated dress is unlikely to leave you feeling suitably gorgeous. Let it go, and should an occasion arise, you have a great excuse to hire or buy a new, stylish one.

Unworn

Items bought for the fantasy life you don't live need to go. Holding onto things you don't ever wear 'just in case' leads to the 'overfull wardrobe and nothing to wear' situation that is so stressful for many women. I'm not going to tell you to get rid of anything you haven't worn in six months, as some things are worn rarely but are worth keeping, but be honest about your current lifestyle and wardrobe needs, and follow your instinct.

Never Worn

Any new item with the tags still on that you have had for more than six months has to go. Don't hold on to it with the misguided thought that one day you will wear it. You won't. Seeing it in the wardrobe with the label still attached only reminds you of the money you've wasted. Give yourself a break and let it go, along with any sense of guilt or shame.

Unwanted Gifts

Let go of any gift of clothing that you never liked, or no longer use. Remember that the gift is in the giving, and it has, therefore, already served its purpose for the person who gave it to you. Give it to charity, or a friend you are sure would love it, so that someone else can make use of it.

Tired and Worn Out

At the other end of the spectrum are the items that you love, or have loved dearly, and are holding onto, despite the fact they have seen better days, i.e. that have worn patches, stains, pulls, holes, are faded, or shiny from over pressing. They need to go. You may be wearing some of the clothes that fall into this category and, therefore, need to keep them for the time being until you replace them. Make sure you note these items as priority purchases and they are at the top of the list when the time comes to *Research* and *Replenish*.

Poor Quality

Bad quality clothes and accessories will never give people the impression that you are a successful woman. In some rare cases, a cheap item can be passed off as good quality, but unless you are a master shopper with a great eye, this is unlikely to be the case. Pay special attention to your shoes, accessories and jewellery, and unless you consciously avoid leather, all your shoes, bags and accessories must be made of real leather. It is often the metal parts and trimmings that give the game away, so ensure your bags and belts have high quality clasps, zips, buckles and fastenings. Let go of any low quality and badly-made items, and believe that you and your career are worth investing more in.

CLIENT STORY

I'd been off work for a year after redundancy from the firm I'd been at for 12 years. It was a fresh start and great opportunity to make an emphatically positive first impression. At 39, I felt that I was at a tipping point; either I moved up in my career now or I stagnated into a lifelong mid-tier manager, which I didn't want to happen.

When I was younger, I managed to carry off wearing average clothes, but as I got older, I felt the rough edge wasn't charming anymore. I started to notice what a difference the right clothes made to women who took care over their appearance.

Everything in my wardrobe was cheap. I'd just pop into a shop, buy something I liked, and that was it. Shopping for clothes was random and I never went looking for a particular item, so I realised I was directionless.

The exercises in Lizzie's process helped me to see my image in a holistic way, as part of my personality, whereas before I'd seen it as completely separate. This took things to another level, and it became more about improving my self-esteem in general, rather than what I'd originally thought it is was about – looking good for my new job.

When I reviewed my wardrobe, I was able to see myself through someone else's eyes, and it wasn't pretty. I actually felt sad about how far away I was from where I wanted to be. I'd previously thought I just needed a helping hand, but once I really started looking at my things I felt like I needed sartorial CPR. However, once my old clothes were out of the house, it felt cathartic and I was really ready for a new wardrobe, and a new start.

When I started my new role, senior people kept telling me how "credible" I was. They didn't really know anything about me, but they already bought into the idea of me as a safe pair of hands because I look poised. What did surprise me was how my younger colleagues responded. They engaged with me and saw me less as one of the 'old crew'. I think this was because my look, though very professional, was fresh and modern and I appeared less distant while still having gravitas.

In the past, I'd felt that wearing nice clothes was a bit vain and ridiculous. But since I upgraded my wardrobe, I now feel like this new, senior role is completely appropriate for me. I feel I have less to prove and I am very relaxed at work, like I don't have to justify my seat at the senior table.

Sentimental

"

OUR MEMORIES ARE WITHIN US, NOT WITHIN OUR THINGS. HOLDING ON TO STUFF IMPRISONS US; LETTING GO IS FREEING.

"

JOSHUA FIELDS MILLBURN

You may have sentimental items of clothing in your wardrobe, your child's first school uniform, or a dress you wore on your first date with your husband, for example.

Consider taking a picture of any item you are holding onto and then let it go. If you can't bear to part with it, store it in a keepsake box out of your wardrobe or, depending on the item, you could frame it or have it where you can see and appreciate it more often.

Doesn't Fit

You must try on every item that hasn't been worn in the last month to make sure it fits and is worth keeping. If you fluctuate in size and have clothes across different sizes, I encourage you to let go of those that haven't fitted you in the last six months.

If they are good quality clothes, which you *honestly* know you'll be able to wear again within the next year, put them on the '*Time Capsule*' pile so they are out of your active wardrobe. (I will explain this in *Reorganise*, which is coming up.)

Fit Issues

Many women are unaware about how their clothes look on their body. There are some clothes that will fit you, as in you can do them up, but they don't fit you *well*. Having clothes that sit and hang correctly, and flatter your shape, will go a long way towards making you looking great, rather than just good.

When clothes don't fit you properly, the unconscious message you give is that you are unaware of yourself, and this lack of attention to detail will have wider implications on how you are perceived at work. Wearing clothes that are too tight can make you appear uptight. Clothes that are a size too big make you look sloppy; people will think you don't care, and that your work will be sloppy. So consider what message every item you try on sends to others.

While going through your wardrobe, thoroughly assess the fit of every item that you plan to keep. Remember, it's easy to have a tailor take in a garment that is a bit big, or take up something that is too long, but harder to let out a garment that is small or lengthen something that is too short. If it's too small, and you are unlikely to be able to wear it in the very near future, let it go. If you love an item, but it's either not sitting or fitting quite right, put it on the alterations pile and get advice from a tailor or seamstress on what can be done. Depending on the garment's quality and the work that would be required, the cost involved can mean it's not worth it, but often, a small alteration to the hem or cuff is all a garment needs to make a big difference to the overall impression you give.

Below are the most common fit issues I come across:

· **CHEST TOO SMALL**

For anything with buttons down the front, such as a shirt or jacket, check the buttons are not pulling open. If you cannot button it up without it pulling at the button, it's too small. If this is something you struggle with, as your chest is large in proportion to your waist, buy a larger size in the future for anything that covers your chest, e.g. a shirt or jacket, and have the waist taken in.

· JACKETS TOO BIG

In a traditional set sleeved, structured jacket, check to see where the shoulder edge sits. If the jacket shoulder comes out further than your shoulder, and the sleeve just below the shoulder looks baggy, it's too big. If there is any sagging of the fabric at the back between the shoulder blades, or around your waist, it is also too big. If the jacket is good quality and one you like in other respects, you can have it tailored to fit.

· SLEEVES TOO LONG

This is the most common fit issue I come across when undertaking a wardrobe review for a petite client. If you usually need your trousers hemmed, your arms are also likely to be proportionally shorter and your sleeves will require the same treatment. Sleeves that are too long and cover the hand down to the knuckles will make you look like a teenager who has been forced to wear a new school blazer they'll need to grow into.

Depending on the style of jacket, consider making the sleeve a 3/4 or bracelet length, which often looks more flattering and feminine, and can completely transform the look. If you are petite, then a three-quarter length sleeves gives the illusion of length, and can therefore make you appear taller.

· SKIRT TOO LONG

A skirt or dress that 'just isn't right' can often be saved from the charity bag by turning the hem up to the knee, or just below the knee. The most flattering length is at the thinnest bit of your leg, which is usually on or just below the knee.

The rare exception to this is a fitted pencil skirt that comes to the calf, and can look gorgeous and slimming when worn with a high heel.

With trousers, the length will depend on the shoe. If you are getting a hem taken up, take the shoes you will most often wear with the item to the tailor so that the length is done correctly to suit the style.

· DRESS TOO SHORT

It is not uncommon for me to ask a client, *"So, where do you wear this?"* as I pull out a short dress from their wardrobe. I assume it is for nights out with friends, only to be told it's for work.

Check that every dress and skirt you wear to work is appropriate in length. If it's too short, it will lessen your gravitas, however great your legs are, and make you appear more junior. Showing too much leg is distracting, and if you are at all self-conscious about it, you will fidget and be constantly pulling at the hem, especially when you sit down and it rises up. So, as a rule of thumb, hems should sit on the knee or just above.

Don't Save Anything for Best

As you go through your items, look at what you own and love, but rarely, if ever, wear. Are these items ones you save as 'for best'? As I've already discussed, many clothes become dated in around five years, so I urge you not to save things for best. When I undertake wardrobe reviews, the most expensive items (made of silk, leather, cashmere, suede) that are saved 'for best' often remain unworn, have become dated, and end up in the charity bag. The day to wear your 'best' clothes seldom comes, so please look out for any item that you are saving and consider how it could be more wearable if you stop viewing it this way. What are you saving it for? Could you wear it on a regular day? See if it could be teamed with a less dressy item, for example, to make it more 'everyday'. Equally, if you are keeping an item because it was an expensive purchase and you have never worn it, and therefore feel guilty about it, let it go.

2.5 THE WARDROBE EDIT

You have now created space for your piles, have bin liners at the ready, and know what to be looking out for. It's time to *Review* and edit your wardrobe.

Go through your wardrobe by clothing categories, and by subcategories, if you have a lot of clothes.

Example clothing categories are:

- CLOTHING CATEGORY: TROUSERS
Subcategories*: Work trousers, short trousers, black trousers, long trousers, summer trousers, etc.*

- CLOTHING CATEGORY: DRESSES
Subcategories*: Work dresses, black dresses, summer dresses, casual dresses, beach dresses, evening dresses, etc.*

- CLOTHING CATEGORY: TOPS
Subcategories: *Fine knitwear, thick jumpers, work tops, blouses, t-shirts, camisoles, etc.*

- TAKE YOUR TIME, BUT DON'T OVERTHINK IT. TRUST YOUR INSTINCTS.

- Pull out ALL your trousers first, pile them up on the bed, and work through them.

- If you have a lot of trousers, divide them further, for example, into jeans or work trousers, summer casual trousers etc.

- Pull out every pair of trousers from every drawer, cupboard, kids' wardrobe, and storage box.

- You need all of the items from a category in one place, because if you have five pairs of black trousers, for example, you need to go through them all at the same time in order to decide which ones are keepers.

- Include *everything* – underwear, shoes, jewellery, accessories, and bags – until it is done.

- If you have a lot of clothes and know this is going to take more time than you have spare to do it in one go, break it down into manageable sessions.

- Make sure you finish up at least a whole category or subcategory, even if it's just a small one, so you can keep track.

- Put items you are keeping back in the wardrobe or

DRAWER, TO BE ORGANISED LATER, AND ITEMS THAT ARE
GOING, OR NEED TO BE DEALT WITH OTHERWISE, ON THEIR
RESPECTIVE PILE.

- EVEN IF YOU LOVE AN ITEM, IT IS WORTH DOUBLE-
CHECKING IT IS RIGHT FOR HOW YOU WANT TO BE SEEN.
IF YOU ARE NOT 100% SURE, CHECK IN WITH YOURSELF
AS TO WHETHER IT CONVEYS YOUR *STYLE WORDS* AND THE
QUALITIES YOU ARE LOOKING TO PROJECT.

The Clothing Queue

When you finish going through the clothing categories, you will have
your 'To Keep' items filling up your wardrobe and drawers again.
Depending how many clothes you had to start with, you may find you
still have a lot of items, many of which are pretty much the same – a
few white shirts, a number of blue jeans, or navy work trousers, for
example.

Imagine that for every category, subcategory, event type or even
level of dress, your items are in a queue. Your favoured item is at the
front of the queue, ready for when its time comes, even if it doesn't
come around very often. Behind it in the queue is your second best
choice (for example, when the first choice is in the wash or at the dry
cleaners). There may be a third, backup option.

With a garment category you wear a lot of, such as work dresses, you may have many very similar items that are all worth keeping. However, with subcategories that are worn less often, you may still have items in the same style or colour that won't ever make it to the front of the queue. If you have four navy skirts, and love three of them, it's unlikely that the other one will ever get worn, so get rid of it.

2.6 REASSESS AND RECONSIDER

- THINK OF EACH ITEM IN A QUEUE WHEN YOU ASSESS ITS PLACE IN A CLOTHING CATEGORY, AND EVEN MORE IMPORTANTLY, IN EACH SUBCATEGORY. WHEN YOU ARE LOOKING AT BLACK OFFICE DRESSES OR A SMART DAY DRESS, LIKE ONE YOU WOULD WEAR TO A WEDDING, WHICH ITEMS WOULD NEVER GET TO THE FRONT OF THE QUEUE? WHEN YOU REACH FOR YOUR JEANS AT THE WEEKEND, WHICH PAIR NEVER GETS CHOSEN OVER THE OTHERS? WHEN YOU HAVE A NIGHT OUT AND WANT TO WEAR HIGH HEELS, WHICH ONES DO YOU NEVER OR RARELY CHOOSE?

I really want to impress on you that 'less is more'. You honestly don't need loads of clothes, and the more you have, the more decisions there are to make, and clothes to organise. When you are only left with the items you love or really like, the more enjoyable and easy your wardrobe becomes. I encourage you to be ruthlessly honest with yourself as you clear out and let go of all the excess.

2.7 MAKE NOTES

As you *Reviewed* and edited your wardrobe, you will gain a clearer idea of what you are working with. Now that you can see what is left in the Keep piles, it is time to start your *Replenish* list. Make a list and take a photo to remind you, if applicable, of the following:

- ITEMS YOU LOVE, BUT THAT HAVE SEEN BETTER DAYS OR NO LONGER FIT.

- ITEMS YOU KNOW ARE MISSING (MAYBE YOU NEED TO REPLACE SOMETHING YOU'VE THROWN OUT) OR WOULD LIKE TO OWN.

- ITEMS THAT ARE REQUIRED TO MAKE AN UNWORN ITEM WEARABLE. TAKE A PHOTO OF THE ITEMS THAT THE NEW PIECE NEEDS TO WORK WITH TO REMIND YOU WHEN YOU ARE *RESEARCHING* OR *REPLENISHING*.

You will come back to add to this list again when you have *Reorganised*, and again when you start your shopping preparation.

2.8 TAKE ACTION

Having a clear out of your wardrobe is cathartic, but you won't feel the benefits of this decluttering exercise until the clothes you aren't keeping are out of the house! Don't leave the bin bags hanging around for weeks, as you will only be tempted to go back into them, and don't put them in another room or in the loft, where they will remain for months.

What I want you to do is:

- Contact anyone who you have in mind for any items, ask if they are interested in them, and let them know how long they have to collect them before they go to charity.

- Take unwanted items to the charity shop or recycling centre.

- Create a listing for any designer items you want to sell on eBay, another resale website, or take them to a resale store.

- Take items to be dry-cleaned and altered at the first opportunity. If it's not done while you're on a roll, they will get forgotten and remain unworn.

Now you have *Reviewed* your wardrobe, it will be much emptier. Seeing what is left after a clear out can often be a shock, and you may see why you have struggled so much. Even if it was full, it wasn't really a full wardrobe; just clothing clutter that clouded the reality of what you actually had to wear and choose from each day.

STEP 2 RECAP

You should now have:

- TAKEN 'BEFORE' PICTURES OF YOUR WARDROBE AND DRAWERS

- REMOVED ANY NON-CLOTHES ITEMS FROM YOUR WARDROBE

- SORTED YOUR CLOTHES INTO SIX PILES: SELL, CHARITY SHOP/FRIEND, RECYCLING, DRY-CLEANING, ALTERATIONS, AND 'TIME CAPSULE'

- UNDERTAKEN A WARDROBE EDIT, CATEGORY BY CATEGORY, SO YOU ARE ONLY LEFT WITH USEFUL ITEMS

- ASSESSED SIMILAR ITEMS TO SEE WHICH NEVER GET WORN

- MADE NOTES TO AID A FUTURE SHOPPING TRIP

Now you can get straight into the next stage – getting *Reorganised*.

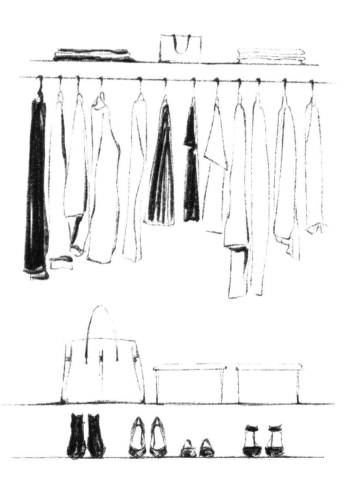

STEP 3 – REORGANISE

Getting dressed and out of the house in the morning can be one of the most stressful and hurried parts of the day, and one that is made much harder when your wardrobe is in disarray. This is unnecessary, a waste of energy, and will soon be a thing of the past.

The role that organisation plays in creating a great image is often overlooked, but it is crucial. Knowing where items of clothing are and having garments that are well looked after and ready to wear when you need them makes getting dressed much easier.

"

FOR EVERY MINUTE SPENT IN ORGANISING,

AN HOUR IS EARNED.

"

BENJAMIN FRANKLIN

The *Review* exercises and the resulting clear out will have reduced the contents of your wardrobe and, therefore, will have already made a noticeable difference. You now know what you own, and that everything you see when you open the wardrobe in the morning will fit, be clean and ready to wear. But to have your mornings run even more smoothly, those items now need to be *Reorganised*.

Hanging

I am a big fan of hanging as much of your wardrobe as possible, because when you see it, you are more likely to wear it. If items are in piles or drawers, they often get forgotten about, and only those at the top of the pile are worn. After wearing and laundering, they are placed on top again, and you repeat the process. When undertaking a wardrobe review, it is often the items uncovered at the bottom that come with the exclamation, "Oh, I'd forgotten I had that!" or "I wondered where that had gone!" When I'm with a client, it isn't uncommon to find two identical garments – one at the back of the drawer that was given up for dead, and its replacement.

Another benefit of hanging is that if you see an item you never wear, you are more likely to get rid of it sooner and free up hanging space for items that you will wear.

With the exception of underwear, sleepwear and gym kit, I advise the hanging of all clothes, if possible. Ensure that the items have enough space to hang freely and remain free of creases. Assuming the hanger is not too wide for the garment, and you wear the item regularly, shoulder 'dents' won't be a problem, even on fine knitwear. Any jersey or knitted items left for a while without being worn can be steamed or dampened to remove any stretching that is caused by the hanger.

3.1 GET HANGING

I. Purchase Hangers

For wardrobe organisation, you need to buy matching hangers. If you went into a shop and everything was hung on different hangers that were all mixed up together, you would walk out and not bother looking. And yet most people encounter this every morning when getting dressed. The look and feel is more akin to a charity shop than a boutique, and the feel of the latter is definitely preferable in your own wardrobe.

I recommend 42 cm velvet slim line hangers. These are brilliant as they take up much less space than other hangers and items stay put without slipping off. These hangers are widely available, and on Amazon and eBay, but make sure to check the size before you buy them as the most widely available are 44 cm and too big if your clothes are less than a UK 12.

Hangers with a formed shoulder, or wooden hangers, if you have some, should be used for jackets, coats and any heavier or structured pieces that require more support on the shoulder.

II. Rehang

Once you have your new hangers, work through your wardrobe and swap out the old hangers for new ones. Do this for your workwear first and then any smart, personal items, leaving the most casual pieces that may currently be in drawers and on shelves until last. By working in this order, you will give priority hanging space to your most important pieces. Remember to make sure your items can hang freely, so that there is space between each hanger, and they are not squashed together.

III. Reorder by Clothing Category

Hanging clothes in a clear and logical order means you can get dressed for work, or pack for a business trip, easily and effortlessly. The right order is down to personal preference, and depends on available space and your lifestyle. The goal is to make it as simple and stress-free as possible – sifting through sundresses and t-shirts while looking for a work blouse or dress is a waste of time. Your wardrobe will evolve and change, so give it a go and see what happens, as your preferred arrangement often becomes apparent over time.

- If you have a distinctly separate business and personal wardrobe, hang them separately so that you will only have to look through the items you need to consider each morning, with no distractions. If there is not a distinct difference between your workwear and personal wear, keep it all together.

- Hang items grouped together in their clothing category, such as trousers, skirts, tops, jackets, and dresses. If you have a lot of items in any category, further divide them into a subcategory in order to finely tune your organisation. For example, tops can be arranged into short sleeved and long sleeved, if that feels right to you.

- If you really want to know what doesn't get worn, turn all your hangers the 'wrong' way, and after wearing an item, turn the hook the 'right' way. After a few months, you will clearly see all the items that you haven't worn.

IV. Organise in Colour Flow

Finally, organise your wardrobe into colour flow order, just like in a brand new box of colour pencils. This way, it is so much easier to locate specific items when you need them, as well as being nice to look at.

- ONCE YOU HAVE GROUPED EACH SET OF ITEMS TOGETHER, REARRANGE THEM WITH THE BLACK ITEMS ON THE LEFT AND WHITE ON THE RIGHT, AND GO THROUGH THE SPECTRUM OF COLOURS AND TONES IN BETWEEN IN WHATEVER WAY FEELS RIGHT TO YOU AND IS VISUALLY PLEASING.

3.2 REORGANISE YOUR DRAWERS

Although I recommend hanging where possible, I also realise this is not practical for everyone. If you do have clothes in drawers, the only way to go is Marie Kondo's method of folding and organising drawers, as made popular in her worldwide bestseller, *The Life-Changing Magic of Tidying*[9]. Rather than pile clothes on top of each other, imagine your clothes like a filing cabinet and 'file' the folded items on their sides in rows, from front to back of the drawers, so you can see every item.

- In order to 'file' the clothes in the drawer, first, you need to fold them in a particular way, with the goal of making a rectangle from your garment.

- First, lay a garment flat; fold its edges into the body to form the long, thin rectangle shape.

- This is then folded in half, and half or a third again (depending on the depth of the drawers and desired size of rectangle), so it can be stood up on its side and won't collapse in your drawer.

Step 1

Step 2

Step 3

Step 4

Step 5

Step 6

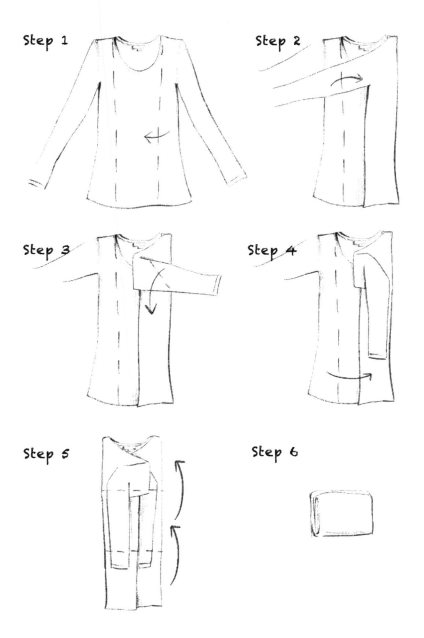

I'll be honest, folding every item using this method takes time, but it will save you much more time in the long run. You can see everything at a glance, pull items out without messing everything else up, and your drawers will stay tidier for longer.

As a bonus, it makes packing a suitcase easy, as you can lift the items you want to take straight out the drawer, without messing everything up, and put them into a suitcase on their sides, seeing them easily.

3.3 STORE 'OFF-SEASON' ITEMS

A reminder that storage should *not* be used as an excuse to hold onto clothes that you don't wear but are scared to let go of. Please don't fall into this trap.

MOST ORGANISING IS NOTHING MORE THAN

WELL-PLANNED HOARDING.

JOSHUA FIELDS MILLBURN

Storage should only be used if you are very short on space, or for off-season items (such as knitwear, tights, and winter coats in the summer, or sundresses, shorts, vest tops in the winter). Unpacking stored items can be an excellent way of reviewing your wardrobe again at the beginning of a new season, seeing what you own, or what will need replacing.

- BEFORE YOU STORE ANY ITEM, REMEMBER TO WASH OR DRY-CLEAN IT, AS FOOD AND PERSPIRATION STAINS YOU CAN'T SEE CAN LEAVE MARKS AND ATTRACT INSECTS AND MOTHS.

- MOVE OFF-SEASON ITEMS INTO EITHER A SECOND WARDROBE, A SEPARATE SET OF DRAWERS, OR STORAGE BOXES THAT ARE SEPARATE FROM YOUR 'ACTIVE WARDROBE'.

- IF SPACE IS TIGHT, USE CLEAR, VACUUM-PACK STORAGE BAGS THAT REDUCE THE CONTENTS TO HALF THE SIZE.

- LABEL THE BAGS OR BOXES WITH A NOTE OF THE CONTENTS CLEARLY VISIBLE. KEEP THEM ACCESSIBLE, SO YOU CAN EASILY LOCATE ANY ITEMS YOU NEED UNEXPECTEDLY OUT OF SEASON, IF YOU GO ON HOLIDAY, FOR EXAMPLE.

3.4 CREATE A TIME CAPSULE

Any items that are too small, but you want to keep and are confident will fit you within a few months, can be stored in what I call a *Time Capsule*. These items are to be revisited next time they are 'in season', or on a date three to six months from now.

- CREATE A DEDICATED STORAGE BOX OR VACUUM STORAGE BAG SPECIFICALLY TO HOLD SUCH ITEMS, KEEPING THEM OUT OF YOUR 'ACTIVE' WARDROBE, AND SEPARATE FROM ANY OFF-SEASON CLOTHES.

- SECURELY STICK A NOTE ON THE BOX, OR CLEARLY VISIBLE INSIDE THE VACUUM BAG, WITH THE CURRENT DATE AND THE DATE YOU WILL REVIEW THE CONTENTS.

- IF THE ITEM STILL DOESN'T FIT ON THE PRE-ASSIGNED DATE, LET IT GO.

3.5 REORGANISE YOUR ACCESSORIES

How you store your accessories will depend on the amount of space you have, and the size and contents of your collection. Hopefully, you have been through them all in your clear out and only good quality items that you love or that fit a purpose now remain.

- WHERE POSSIBLE, STORE ITEMS SO YOU CAN SEE THEM.

- FIT SMALL RAILS INSIDE YOUR WARDROBE DOORS, OR HOOKS SOMEWHERE ACCESSIBLE. HANG YOUR SCARVES, BELTS AND NECKLACES, AS YOU WILL RARELY USE THEM IF THEY ARE BURIED IN A DRAWER.

- EARRINGS, RINGS, AND BRACELETS NEED PUTTING IN ORDER AND IN CLEAR BOXES, OR DIVIDED INTO COMPARTMENTS WHERE YOU CAN SEE WHAT YOU HAVE AT A GLANCE.

- IF YOU HAVE VALUABLE JEWELLERY THAT REQUIRES A SAFE, TAKE PICTURES OF THE ITEMS AND STICK THESE INSIDE YOUR WARDROBE, SO YOU CAN SEE AT A GLANCE WHAT YOU OWN, AND MAYBE YOU'LL BE INSPIRED TO WEAR THEM MORE OFTEN WHEN GETTING READY.

- IF POSSIBLE, GET SHOES OUT OF THEIR SHOEBOXES AND STORE THEM WHERE YOU CAN SEE THEM. USE CLEAR STORAGE BOXES OR SHOE RAILS. DON'T HAVE A PILE OF SHOES IN THE BOTTOM OF THE WARDROBE.

- IF YOU DO WANT TO KEEP YOUR SHOES IN THEIR ORIGINAL BOXES, STICK PHOTOS ON THE OUTSIDE, OR ON THE INSIDE OF THE WARDROBE, SO YOU ARE REMINDED DAILY OF YOUR OPTIONS.

- INVEST IN SHOE AND BOOT TREES TO KEEP SHOES IN GOOD CONDITION.

3.6 TAKE STOCK

Now you have *Reviewed* and *Reorganised* your wardrobe, I want you to take stock of what is left, which is much easier now that you have everything neatly organised. Often, after a big wardrobe clear out, it is surprising to find that there are actually many items that do work and project the right image. They were just hidden amongst the clutter. So, even before you've bought anything new, your image may already be greatly improved!

Now, you can take stock and find out how far off the mark you really are.

- COUNT WHAT YOU HAVE LEFT, CATEGORY BY CATEGORY; HOW MANY SUITS, OR SKIRTS, FOR EXAMPLE. NOTE THE TOTAL FOR EACH CATEGORY. IF THERE ARE STILL QUITE A FEW, FURTHER DIVIDE INTO SUBCATEGORIES TO GET A CLEARER PICTURE. REMEMBER NOT TO COUNT ANY TIRED OR WORN ITEMS THAT ARE ONLY REMAINING THERE TEMPORARILY UNTIL THEY ARE REPLACED.

- WHAT IS OBVIOUSLY LACKING? WHAT DO YOU BUY EASILY AND THEREFORE HAVE LOTS OF?

- TAKE PHOTOS OF YOUR WARDROBE AGAIN, AS YOU DID BEFORE YOU STARTED. COMPARE THE 'BEFORE AND AFTER PICTURES' AND CONGRATULATE YOURSELF ON A JOB WELL DONE!

- ADD A NOTE OF ANY FURTHER ITEMS YOU FEEL ARE MISSING AND NEED PRIORITISING.

STEP 3 RECAP

You should now have:

- PURCHASED MATCHING VELVET HANGERS AND REHUNG AS MUCH OF YOUR WARDROBE AS POSSIBLE

- *REORGANISED* YOUR WARDROBE INTO CLOTHING CATEGORY, SUBCATEGORY AND COLOUR FLOW ORDER

- *REORGANISED* YOUR DRAWERS

- STORED 'OFF-SEASON' ITEMS AND CREATED A *TIME CAPSULE* FOR ANYTHING THAT DOESN'T QUITE FIT

- *REORGANISED* YOUR ACCESSORIES

- TAKEN STOCK OF WHAT YOU HAVE, CREATED A LIST OF WHAT'S MISSING, AND TAKEN AN 'AFTER' PHOTO OF YOUR CLOTHES, BEAUTIFULLY ORGANISED

- CONGRATULATED YOURSELF ON A JOB WELL DONE!

Once you are done, we are ready to begin looking forward and can start thinking about the new possibilities of your wardrobe that await you.

STEP 4 – RETHINK

Having gained a clearer idea of your preferences and your general requirements, as well as which specific items you need, there is one more step you need to take before you can *Research* and *Replenish* your wardrobe.

To make your wardrobe as effortless as possible, you are going to *Rethink* it, and begin to plan what your new wardrobe may look like.

Taking what you have discovered in the previous steps, you can begin to plan your new wardrobe. However, there are a few key factors you also need to think about. You now need to consider your colour palette, how to project your *Qualities*, and what you wear and therefore need in your wardrobe. You will also need to think about putting all this together, in order to create your own signature style and learn how to build a collection of clothes that will all work together.

The points discussed in this *Rethink* step all interconnect and build upon each other. They are not linear as written, so it is important to read through them all before answering the questions in the individual activities.

Colour

It is not possible for me to go into colour in detail in this book, as attempting to explain and describe something in black and white that is visual and colourful is pretty impossible! My purpose here is to give you some pointers to consider and explore for yourself. If you would like to find out what colours suit you best, I encourage you to have your colours done by a trained colour consultant, but even then, please don't be a slave to any palette you are given — only use it as a guide.

Choose a Colour Palette

When creating an effortless wardrobe, deciding on a colour palette makes it so much easier. It reduces your options when researching and shopping, as you'll know without much thought if an item coordinates with everything else.

Your wardrobe's colour palette will comprise of three elements:

- NEUTRAL COLOURS, WHICH ARE YOUR STAPLE BACKGROUND COLOURS

- KEY COLOURS, WHICH WILL MAKE UP THE BULK OF YOUR OUTFITS

- ACCENT COLOURS, WHICH YOU WILL USE SPARINGLY TO GIVE A LIFT TO YOUR OUTFITS

Neutral Colours

Your *Neutral Colours* are the lighter, background colours, which you will use for *Core* pieces (to be explained shortly), as well as accessories, such as shoes and bags.

Your *Neutrals* palette will depend on your personal colouring, your contrast levels (how much light and dark you have in your colouring), and the impression you need to project.

Your options are: white, ivory, cream, sand, light grey, blush, nude and the colour of your hair. They can sometimes be the same as *Key Colours* – light grey or sand, for example.

Key Colours

Your *Key Colours* are your wardrobe's anchor. These are the main colours of your business wardrobe – the colours that you prefer to wear at work. Your choice will depend on your own colouring, personal style, the industry you work in, as well as the *Qualities* you want to project.

For business, it is highly likely that your first choice will be either black or navy. Other business options include: charcoal, burgundy, royal blue, bottle green, light grey, camel, sand, blush, or ivory.

In theory, you can have any colour as a *Key Colour*, so if you work in a creative field, are dramatic and confident, you could have red, pink or cobalt blue, for example, but generally, they are better left as *Accent Colours*.

Accent Colours

Your *Accent Colours* are the colourful, more standout colours, which are rarely worn from head to toe. In business, they feature in small doses, in one or two items at a time, from a dress for the biggest impact, to a bracelet or shoe for a pop of colour.

Accent Colours will predominately feature in the *Character Pieces* (explained later in this chapter) of your wardrobe. Their purpose is to add interest to an outfit in an item or accessory, and so they *must* work with at least one of your *Key Colours* and your *Neutral Colours*, but more if possible.

In business and professional attire, the *Accent Colours* are most often jewel shades of blues and greens or bright shades of pinks and reds.

4.1 RESEARCH YOUR NEUTRAL, KEY, AND ACCENT COLOURS

This exercise aims to get a sense of which colours you like, and then see how they work together as a palette, which will anchor your wardrobe and guide your purchases when you *Replenish*.

Seeing colours will inspire you, and pinning them helps you to see what they look like together.

Ultimately, you will create a palette of 8-15 colours: 2-3 *Neutral Colours*, 1-3 *Key Colours* (two dark with another lighter colour, for warmer weather perhaps, which may be the same as one of your *Neutrals*), and 5-8 *Accent Colours*.

- CREATE TWO NEW PINTEREST BOARDS, ONE FOR *KEY/NEUTRALS*, AS THEY ARE SIMILAR AND OFTEN CROSS OVER, AND ONE FOR *ACCENTS*.

- START TO COLLECT IMAGES OF THE COLOURS YOU ARE CONSIDERING, AND PIN THEM ON THE APPROPRIATE BOARD.

- THE IMAGES CAN BE JUST OF THE COLOUR AND DON'T HAVE TO BE OF CLOTHES IN THAT COLOUR. TYPE IN AS ACCURATE A DESCRIPTION OF THE COLOUR YOU WANT TO FIND AS POSSIBLE, I.E. 'COBALT', 'MAGENTA', 'TEAL', OR ADD 'DARK', 'BRIGHT', 'PALE', OR 'LIGHT' TO THE COLOUR NAME.

- LOOK AT YOUR EXISTING PINTEREST BOARDS AND YOUR *INSPIRATION BOARD* TO SEE WHAT THE COLOUR THEMES WERE OR WHICH COLOURS CAME UP, THEN MAKE A NOTE AND ADD ANY RELEVANT PHOTOS TO YOUR NEW BOARDS BY 'RE-PINNING' THEM ON YOUR NEW *KEY/NEUTRALS* OR *ACCENTS* BOARDS.

- SEARCH PINTEREST FOR COLOUR PALETTE INSPIRATION AND IDEAS, AND FIND IMAGES OF OUTFIT COMBINATION COLOURS THAT YOU LIKE. SEARCH 'BURNT ORANGE COLOUR PALETTE' OR 'NAVY COLOUR PALETTE'.

- AS THE BOARDS BEGIN TO FILL UP WITH COLOUR, YOU WILL BEGIN TO SEE WHAT COLOURS LOOK LIKE WITH EACH OTHER, AND CAN THEN BEGIN TO SEE A POTENTIAL PALETTE MATERIALISE.

- DELETE ANY COLOURS THAT FALL FROM FAVOUR OR DON'T WORK WITH OTHERS IN THE PALETTE.

This process will evolve as you go through the remaining steps. When you *Research*, look at the available colours and see what you are drawn to.

Finally, a note of caution here – I am not saying you *have* to wear colour. You may be someone whose outfits are devoid of any *Accent Colours*, and are based solely on a *Neutral* and *Key* palette. That is absolutely fine. I have had a number of clients who have felt that on reaching a certain age, they 'should' start wearing bright jackets or statement necklaces. They felt a huge relief when I reassured them that was not the case, and if they wanted to wear only navy and keep it low-key, that was fine. A monochrome look, with varying shades of white, grey and black, or pale blues through to navy, can look fantastic. Or you may prefer to create an understated look with only a tiny accent of colour, such as a trim or accessory. Always dress in colours that feel right for you, that you feel good in and enjoy wearing. However, if you haven't experimented with how different colours look on you, I really encourage you to have a go at trying out some new colours when you come to *Research*, and just see how they feel.

Projecting Your Qualities

As in the case of colour, there is no one-size-fits-all answer when it comes to *Qualities* and *Style Words*, and therefore, your personal style. There are many unique *Qualities*, and what one woman chooses for her career may be totally different to those deemed important or preferable by another.

However, to get you started and give you some ideas, here are a few of the *Qualities* that I have found to be consistently desirable among many of my clients who are leaders, along with my suggestions on how to dress to convey them.

Approachable

If you are a leader who wants to be known for being open and approachable, you need to make sure that your image reflects this. As a classically corporate look is a high contrast outfit that appears authoritative – a white shirt and dark suit, for example – wearing a lower contrast combination will make you look more approachable. This could perhaps be a mid-toned blue suit with an off-white silk blouse instead. Wear softer, more tactile fabrics, such as silk or jersey. Wearing a top in the colour of your eyes will also help with personal connection, as it draws attention to them and creates an opportunity for eye contact.

Authentic

To look authentic, you need to look natural and comfortable in what you are wearing. So ensure that the make-up you wear enhances your appearance and looks real, rather than creating a mask. Too much foundation or heavy eye make-up and an obvious reliance on fake tan, false nails, fillers and Botox will not help you to come across as authentic.

Competent

If you don't look like you have the required skills, knowledge and experience, it's going to be hard for others to trust that you do. Ensure your dress is appropriate for your industry, and matches the level of competency that you wish to signal. If you are young for your level of expertise, dress more senior. This does not mean becoming frumpy, but you can impart a feeling of being more experienced by ensuring that you wear the best quality clothes you can, and shopping at the same level as someone who is older in your position would shop.

Forward-Thinking

If you are in an industry where being perceived as 'forward-thinking' is desirable, such as manufacturing, technology or science, it is essential that your wardrobe reflects current trends.

This does not mean that you have to be a slave to the latest fashion, but having a modern style will show others that you are in step with change, and know what's going on in the world. Wearing dated clothes is ageing and can signal that your ideas are outdated too.

Professional

Because the desire to look professional spans all industries and levels, the styles of 'professional' clothing can vary greatly. However, there are some constant factors. Clothes must be of good quality and clean, with no stains, holes, or creases, and not be overwashed or out of shape. Shoes should be in a good state, and not over-worn or scuffed. Everything should fit well without either pulling or sagging, and be appropriate for your age, body shape and seniority. Outfits should be work appropriate; skirts and dresses not too short, heels not too high, and tops not too revealing, so that they show too much cleavage, all of which is distracting and looks unprofessional.

Trustworthy

Having a consistent image is an important part of assuring people that you can be relied upon. Making sure you look well put together every single day means you are ready to step in and step up when called upon. People can trust you will deliver when your wardrobe signals that you are always ready to go, whereas when one day you look put together and another thrown together, they cannot.

CLIENT STORY

CATALYST FOR WARDROBE UPGRADE

Growing a business

I'd worked as a freelance consultant, but now wanted to scale up and take my business to the next level and felt that an image overhaul would help me get into the right headspace.

I needed an image that would be smart enough to appeal to my corporate clients, but cool and creative enough to appeal to the agencies and younger businesses I also work with. I needed a wardrobe that was flexible – taking me easily from school run to client meeting to working from home.

Going through the exercises helped me think about how I wanted to be seen and made me realise that I wanted to express more of my personality through my style – something I had been failing at big time.

It was great to do the Inspiration Board, as through it, I stumbled across a very clear direction of where I wanted to go with my style. After that, I was able to review my existing wardrobe, and it was a great way to see my clothes with fresh eyes. I hadn't noticed how tired looking some of my pieces were, and where the gaps were.

The day after shopping, I was late for work because I got so many compliments about my outfit on the school run! Friends have commented that I've found my mojo and I have never felt happier with how I look.

Upgrading my wardrobe and working on my image felt like a big investment of time and money at the time, but I've reaped huge rewards since.

The new wardrobe was just the beginning. It gave me confidence to grow my business. I felt I looked the part, so it was just a matter of getting my business to catch up. It is now flourishing and my image upgrade was definitely a key part in kick-starting that process.

Here I am, in my forties, feeling more confident, stylish and powerful than I ever did in my twenties. I feel I can express myself so much better through my image. Now 'what you see is what you get', whereas before, my slightly dowdy image didn't convey the sparky, creative person that I am.

4.2 PROJECTING YOUR QUALITIES

• READ THROUGH YOUR *QUALITIES* AND *STYLE WORDS* FROM STEP 1 AND *REFLECT*. HAVE A THINK ABOUT EACH ONE AND WRITE DOWN THE WAYS THAT YOU FEEL YOU COULD PROJECT THEM, USING YOUR CLOTHES AND IMAGE.

• IF THERE ARE WORDS THAT YOU ARE UNSURE OF HOW TO PROJECT, TRY THINKING OF SOMEONE IN THE PUBLIC EYE WHO YOU FEEL PROJECTS THOSE *QUALITIES* WELL. FIND PICTURES OF THEM, AND CONSIDER HOW THEY USE THEIR CLOTHES AND IMAGE TO IMPART THEM.

What Do You Really Wear?

You are now going to work out what you actually need from your wardrobe on a day-to-day basis.

Few women stop to consider how they spend their time at work, and therefore, which clothes will enable them to have a functioning and wearable wardrobe. Noting your actual wardrobe requirements over a number of weeks will not only give you clarity, but also show how often you wear a different level of dress. This information will allow you to build a wardrobe that reflects your current needs, rather than a past or fantasy life.

I want you to consider these four *Levels of Dress* in your business wardrobe. Take a moment to familiarise yourself with them now, as you'll be using them for the next exercise.

- LEVEL 1: QUALITY CASUAL – I.E. GOOD QUALITY JEANS, JUMPERS, T-SHIRTS, SMART TRAINERS.

- LEVEL 2: SMART CASUAL – I.E. SMART COTTON TROUSERS, FINE KNIT SWEATERS, POINTED FLAT SHOES.

- LEVEL 3: BUSINESS CASUAL – I.E. SMART SEPARATES, SUCH AS SILK BLOUSES, TROUSERS, SKIRTS, JACKETS, JERSEY DRESSES, LOW HEELS.

- LEVEL 4: BUSINESS FORMAL – I.E. SUITS, STRUCTURED DRESSES, JACKETS, HIGH HEELS.

4.3 YOUR WORK WARDROBE REQUIREMENTS

Let's find out how often you need outfits from each different level.

- LOOK IN YOUR DIARY FOR A RECENT TWO-WEEK PERIOD THAT SHOWS A TYPICAL EXAMPLE OF YOUR WORKING LIFE. TWO WEEKS IS USUALLY THE IDEAL TIMEFRAME

AND THE MINIMUM THAT YOU WILL WANT TO CREATE A WARDROBE FOR WHEN YOU *REPLENISH*. HOWEVER, IF YOUR WORKWEAR REQUIREMENTS DIFFER WEEK BY WEEK, I SUGGEST YOU LOOK AT A FOUR-WEEK TIMEFRAME TO GAIN AN ACCURATE OVERVIEW, OR IF MOST DAYS AND WEEKS ARE MUCH THE SAME, A WEEK MAY BE ENOUGH.

- TURN TO A FRESH PAGE OF YOUR NOTEBOOK, OR OPEN A FRESH DIGITAL NOTE. WRITE THE *LEVELS OF DRESS* NUMBERS 1 TO 4 IN A COLUMN DOWN THE LEFT SIDE OF YOUR PAGE.

- GO THROUGH YOUR DIARY AND HOW YOU SPENT THE WORKING DAY AS BEST YOU CAN. NEXT TO THE APPROPRIATE LEVEL OF DRESS, WRITE THE WORK SITUATION IN THE SECOND COLUMN. THEN PUT A TALLY MARK IN A THIRD COLUMN, AND ADD TO IT WITH EACH SUBSEQUENT OCCURRENCE.

- REMEMBER, SOME DAYS YOU MAY DRESS ACROSS MORE THAN ONE LEVEL; FOR EXAMPLE, HAVING PRESENTED AT A CONFERENCE IN THE MORNING (LEVEL 4), YOU THEN CHANGE TO CATCH A LONG-HAUL FLIGHT (LEVEL 2).

- WHEN YOU HAVE BEEN THROUGH YOUR DIARY FOR TWO WEEKS, ADD IT ALL UP AND WRITE THE TOTAL FOR EACH *LEVEL OF DRESS* IN A FOURTH COLUMN.

Worked example of a two-week period/10 days:

Dress Level	Situation	Score	Level Total
1	Working from home	II	2
2	Travelling long-haul	II	
	An offsite away day	I	3
3	Networking event	II	
	Regular days at office	IIII	6
4	Delivering a Keynote Speech	I	
	Offsite New Client Meeting	II	
	Presentation to the Board	I	4

TOTAL WEARS 15

· NEXT, CALCULATE THE PERCENTAGE FOR EACH *LEVEL OF DRESS* BY USING A CALCULATOR TO DIVIDE EACH *LEVEL TOTAL* BY THE NUMBER OF *TOTAL WEARS*. ONCE YOU HAVE GOT A FIGURE, MOVE THE DECIMAL POINT 2 PLACES TO THE RIGHT TO OBTAIN THE PERCENTAGE. KEEP THESE PERCENTAGES HANDY, AS YOU WILL REFER TO THEM LATER WHEN YOU *RESEARCH* AND *REPLENISH*.

Level of Dress	Level Totals	%Use
1	2	(2*15 = 0.13) 13%
2	3	(3*15 = 0.2) 20%
3	6	(6*15 = 0.4) 40%
4	4	(4*15= 0.26) 26%

This does not need to be super precise. Your aim is to clarify what you need in your business wardrobe and see how your current wardrobe measures up so that you know where the gaps are.

The Advantages of Having a Signature Style

Many successful businesspeople have a signature style, and swear by wearing the same clothes every day, and that doesn't just mean wearing a suit: Mark Zuckerberg, Barack Obama, Richard Branson, and even fashion designer Karl Lagerfeld wear pretty much the same clothes every day, and by doing this have created a signature style and the recognisable visual asset of their personal brand.

Facebook CEO, Mark Zuckerberg, explained how even small decisions, like choosing what to wear could be tiring and consume energy, and why he didn't want to waste any time on it, by saying, "I really want to clear my life to make it so that I have to make as few decisions as possible about anything except how to best serve this community."[10]

Barack Obama, echoed this in a *Vanity Fair* interview, where he stated, "You'll see I wear only grey or blue suits. I'm trying to pare down decisions. I don't want to make decisions about what I'm eating or wearing. Because I have too many other decisions to make."[11]

And research backs this up. It's known as 'decision fatigue'[12]. Scientists have found you can't make decision after decision without running low on mental energy. The more choices you need to make over the course of a day, the harder it becomes for your brain, so by taking one more decision away (by wearing the same clothes), you reserve mental capacity for other, more important decisions.

Creating a signature style, even if not wearing entirely the same look every day, is a tactic that is also used by many prominent women. Female politicians like Nicola Sturgeon, Hillary Clinton, and Angela Merkel[13], along with high profile women, such as Ellen DeGeneres and Anna Wintour, wear predictable and repeatable looks on a day-to-day basis. This frees up headspace, enabling them to focus on the demands of their day.

Creating Your Signature Style

Whether you are short on time, disinterested in clothes or just feel that you could do with one less decision every day, having a signature style is a great tactic.

When you have a signature look, you will not only feel confident about what you wear, but also won't need to think about it. You'll save money and time by not buying items that you never wear, and you'll only look for items that fall within certain pre-determined parameters when you are shopping. As a bonus, you will create a visually consistent personal brand.

TO HAVE STYLE IS TO HAVE

FEELING FOR WHAT IS CURRENTLY

FASHIONABLE, AND STILL TO

SIMULTANEOUSLY REMAIN TRUE TO ONESELF!

HUBERT DE GIVENCHY

The variety of options that make it so much harder for women to dress for work compared to men can actually be used to your advantage when creating your 'uniform' or signature style.

It takes a bit of thought to put your signature style together, and you may have to play around with different ideas before you find what works for you, but it will save you time and energy in the long run.

Although I suggest you set some style boundaries, it doesn't have to be boring. Something about your daily outfit will remain the same, but the colours, styles or fabrics can change to whatever degree you choose.

For example, your signature style could simply mean wearing the same colour, or combination of colours. Or it may be that you only wear dresses, or always wear a slim-fitted trouser and a blazer with bright scarves or silk blouses.

Your 'uniform' does not have to be obvious, or something that anyone else would even notice. If you only wear trousers and a top or jacket, for example, it's a formula that you know, which makes shopping and dressing easier.

You may stick to just one formula with little change, and wear the same combination of items or a particular colour or combination of colours, for example, but for variety, I suggest you create more than one formula. Your formula might be a Colour Formula, or a Trouser Formula or a Dress Formula. Some people will only have one formula, but you should have no more than three.

Below are a few examples of classic formulas, just to get you started.

A *Colour Formula* could be either:

- Only wear black with white

- Only wear navy with cream

A *Trousers Formula* could be either:

- Trousers + Jacket + Silk t-shirt + Heel

- Trousers + Top + Flats

A *Dress Formula* could be either:

- Sleeved dress + Statement Necklace + Heel

- Dress + Jacket + Heel

It is quite likely you are using a loose formula already. If so, it can be upgraded or tweaked to align with your ambitions.

If you tend to wear or Dress + Cardigan + Heels, for example, swap the cardigans for more structured jackets, or try wearing dresses with sleeves so that a cardigan is not required.

Or if you often tend to wear Black Trousers + Shirt + Flats, your upgrade could be to try a new style of trouser in a different colour or texture, with a silk blouse and a heel.

4.4 CREATE YOUR SIGNATURE STYLE FORMULA

When you consciously decide to wear a specific combination, or formula, shopping and dressing becomes easier. Knowing your preferred look, and which combinations you already gravitate to, is a good place to start. Answer the following questions and make notes:

- TO CREATE YOUR SIGNATURE STYLE FORMULA, FIRST LOOK TO YOUR PREVIOUS OR CURRENT 'GO-TO' OUTFIT COMBINATIONS. ARE THERE ANY REOCCURRING LOOKS OR COMBINATIONS THAT YOU NATURALLY PUT TOGETHER?

- WHY DO YOU WEAR THEM? IS IT BECAUSE THEY MAKE YOU FEEL GREAT, OR BECAUSE YOU ALWAYS BUY THE SAME THING OUT OF HABIT?

- YOUR AESTHETIC PREFERENCES HOLD CLUES TO YOUR INSTINCTIVE STYLE. GO BACK TO YOUR PINTEREST BOARDS, AND ANY NOTES YOU MADE WHEN REVIEWING THE BOARDS.

Can you see a way that you could wear the items already in your wardrobe differently?

- Consider any style formulas you already use, and ask what you can do to update or upgrade them.

- Write down 1-3 signature style formulas and the pieces required to create them.

The Two Types of Clothing

A successful wardrobe combines a number of interrelated pieces that all work together, but that only happens with careful planning, consideration and shopping. To help simplify things further, consider your wardrobe as being made up of two types of clothing, *Core* and *Character Pieces*, which can be easily mixed and matched to become an effortless, put together wardrobe.

Core Pieces

These are your plain or understated garments, e.g. silk t-shirt, tights, dresses, jackets, trousers, and any other staple items at the heart of your signature style that can be mixed and matched easily together in different combinations.

Character Pieces

These are your interesting highlight pieces, e.g. coloured dress, blouse with coloured buttons, which add the variety, detail, excitement and personality to your signature style. It is crucial that *Character Pieces* can be easily combined with many of your *Core Pieces*; otherwise, they will remain unworn.

Core Pieces Explained

Core Pieces are the foundation, and form the bulk of your wardrobe. They need to be easy to mix and match, and relate to each other in an overall consistent style. They are understated, and in your *Key and Neutral Colours*. These include: jumpers, blouses, trousers, jackets and dresses, and shoes, etc. *Core Pieces* may vary in style; necklines, cuts, lengths, etc., depending on *your* personal style preferences.

At least one *Core Piece* in each category of clothing needs to be *totally* plain, then other pieces can have a more interesting design, shape, or styling details; for example, a navy dress with a zip going down the back, or with a bow at the neck.

These pieces won't go with absolutely everything, but they are still understated in design, and the workhorses you will rely on, day in, day out. They will counter balance *Character Pieces* that would otherwise be too much for a particular day, and you'll want them to last a few years of regular wear, so it's worth investing.

> "
>
> SIMPLICITY IS THE ULTIMATE
> FORM OF SOPHISTICATION.
>
> "
>
> **LEONARDO DI VINCI**

Unfortunately, it's not possible for me to give a definitive 'must have' or 'essentials' list without knowing your style or your role. However, there are the items that I find work again and again in most business wardrobes, whatever the style preference and the business environment. This is a guide to help you start to think about which *Core Pieces* you need. Of course, what you require will depend on your signature style.

The choice of colour depends on your chosen *Key and Neutral* palettes. If something is listed that you wouldn't wear, you don't have to buy it! This is only intended for guidance.

- Ivory silk or fine fabric t-shirts, camisoles or vests

- Nude camisoles or a vest for wearing underneath silk blouses or fine sweaters

- Fine knit sweaters in cream, grey, navy, and/or black

- 5-10 blouses/tops

- 1 suit/mix & match combination of a jacket, trousers, dress or skirt

- 1 tweed/boucle/textured jacket in a *Key Colour*, and/or another in an *Accent Colour* (making it a *Character Piece* that is easy to combine)

- 2-3 pairs of trousers/skirts

- 2-3 dresses

- Flats in black, nude, tan, and/or brown

- Heels in black, nude, and/or tan

- 1 lightweight overcoat/trench coat in black, camel or navy

- 1 KNEE-LENGTH WOOLLEN WINTER COAT IN EITHER BLACK, CAMEL, NAVY AND/OR GREY

- 1 STRUCTURED LEATHER WORK BAG IN BLACK AND/OR NAVY

- 1 CASHMERE SHAWL/WRAP IN BLACK, CAMEL AND/OR NAVY

4.5 LIST YOUR CORE REQUIREMENTS

- LOOK AGAIN AT YOUR PERCENTAGES AND WHAT YOU NEED IN YOUR WARDROBE TO SEE WHICH LEVEL OF DRESS YOU PREDOMINANTLY WEAR, AND ENSURE YOUR *CORE PIECES* COVER THIS AS A PRIORITY.

- CHECK WHICH PIECES YOU ALREADY OWN, AND THEN MAKE A NOTE OF ANY MISSING PIECES THAT ARE REQUIRED TO FILL THE GAPS.

- KEEP THIS LIST TO HAND AS YOU WILL NEED IT WHEN YOU BEGIN YOUR *RESEARCH*.

Character Pieces Explained

Character Pieces are the interesting items: highly styled, fashionable, eye-catching, coloured, patterned, or embellished. They add daily variety and interest to your *Core Pieces*, and create the look of your signature style. They don't need to match them with other *Character Pieces*, but they *must* be wearable with your *Core Pieces*.

In a small, wearable wardrobe, *Character Pieces* should only make up a small percentage of your clothes. If you prefer an understated look, then you may have very few, but if you love standing out and having more variety, you will have more.

Most people fall into the trap of having too many *Character Pieces* and not enough *Core Pieces*, which leads to an overfull wardrobe and nothing to wear, and also makes putting outfits together difficult. This usually comes about because the items that catch your eye while walking through a shop or browsing online are the ones that shout the loudest, grab your attention, and are generally more fun to try and buy. Be cautious, at least until you have first bought all the *Core Pieces* you require.

Character Pieces are often the more fashion-led items, so have less longevity. Only buy a *Character Piece* if you own an equivalent *Core Piece* already, i.e. don't buy a leopard print coat unless you already own one in your *Key Colour*, i.e. black or navy. Be sensible.

This is a guide to help you start to think about which *Character Pieces* you need, but precisely what you require will depend on your signature style.

Remember, a *Character Piece* is not necessarily attention grabbing or brightly coloured, but is instead anything with a bit 'extra', such as a trim or a style detail etc., that makes it less easy to wear or go with everything.

If you have a quiet and understated signature style, your *Character Pieces* may have just subtle hints, e.g. a coloured shoe or bracelet, and so you may not require many *Character* clothing pieces at all.

- 5 -10 TOPS

- 2-3 TROUSERS/SKIRTS

- 2-5 DRESSES

- 1-2 COATS

- 1-2 JACKETS

- 1-2 BAGS

- 2-5 PAIRS OF SHOES

- 2-10 ITEMS OF JEWELLERY

4.6 LIST DESIRABLE CHARACTER PIECES

Until you have a few basic and understated *Core Pieces* in place, I don't want you to buy any *Character Pieces*, but you can still start to make notes about what you would like to find and what you already know you need.

- By looking at your Pinterest boards, and considering the *Accent Colours* you feel you'd like to try out, make a note of any items you would like to find, and in which colours, i.e. a red suede heel, or a cream lace top or leopard print flats.

Underwear Essentials

Regardless of your style, every professional woman also needs the following core underwear pieces:

Seam-Free Nude Bra

A seam-free nude bra is a wardrobe essential, so I insist if you don't own one, buying one is a priority. I don't want you to be a smartly-dressed woman with clothes that look puckered and lumpy due to your bra seams or lace. Nude is a must if you are wearing white or ivory silk tops or blouses. If your underwear is at all noticeable to others, it gives the impression that you lack self-awareness.

Seam-Free Knickers

Wearing seam-free knickers is essential for many outfits. You can get virtually invisible 'laser cut' shorts in most stores and brands, so there is no excuse to have a VPL or wear a thong. Lumps and bumps that are visible are not the fault of your body but your underwear. The indent lines are caused by the digging in of elastic, so make sure your tights and knickers come high enough over your tummy not to leave a line across your stomach, and look for styles that are specially designed to leave a smooth silhouette.

Shapewear

Shapewear is not about sucking and holding you in to make you smaller, but to create clean, smooth lines that make all the difference to how an outfit looks. You can find shapewear in most lingerie departments, at all price points, and it is important to find the right item for your shape and the garment you will be wearing it under.

Tights

Not everyone wears skirts and dresses, but if you do then good quality tights are on your essentials list. With tights, you get what you pay for, so if you haven't done so already, now is the time to ditch the 3 packs from Boots. Buy from high quality brands, get a couple of pairs to try them out first, and consider the cost per wear ratio if you think they are expensive. You will be a convert once you feel the difference in the fit and quality, and they will last you much longer too.

4.7 UNDERWEAR UPGRADE

You will need to get the right underwear before you start shopping. It can make a difference to your shape, and as a result, the fit of clothes and how they look. Good underwear is worth the investment. It's probably worn more than any other item you own, so a quick calculation of the cost per wear on even a seemingly expensive bra, pair of support pants or tights will help you to see it is a very worthwhile investment.

- LIST THE UNDERWEAR ESSENTIALS YOU FEEL YOU REQUIRE AND MAKE A NOTE OF THE GAPS TO BE FILLED.

- I INSIST THAT IF YOU HAVEN'T DONE SO IN THE LAST 6 MONTHS, YOU FIRST GET PROFESSIONALLY FITTED FOR A BRA, AND PREFERABLY AT A SPECIALIST SHOP. I RECOMMEND YOU DO THIS BEFORE YOU START TRYING ON NEW ITEMS, AS IT CAN MAKE QUITE A DIFFERENCE TO HOW YOUR CLOTHES LOOK AND FIT. MANY LINGERIE BOUTIQUES ARE OWNED AND RUN BY EXPERTS WHO KNOW EVERYTHING THERE IS TO KNOW ABOUT BRAS. AS A RULE, YOU WANT TO GO TO A STORE THAT WILL 'FIT' YOU, NOT 'MEASURE' YOU.

UNFORTUNATELY, DEPARTMENT STORES CAN BE HIT AND MISS, DEPENDING ON THE MEMBER OF STAFF. IF THE FIRST THING AN ASSISTANT DOES IS PULL OUT A TAPE MEASURE, RATHER THAN VISUALLY ASSESS YOU IN YOUR BRA, PLEASE MAKE AN EXCUSE AND GO ELSEWHERE.

How to Build Outfits

It's one thing to have a wardrobe of great items, but often, it's putting them together that can be the tricky bit.

One of the common mistakes to avoid is building an outfit that is jarring and therefore a distraction. You want people to be listening to you and not contemplating the thought process behind what you have on, and wondering if you looked in the mirror this morning.

The most common reason that outfits don't look put together is because items in the outfit don't relate to each other. The most important consideration when building outfits is making sure there is a connection between the separate pieces in some way, such as a similar style, matching colour or they are coordinated. Another issue is when either an outfit or item is unsuitable for the situation or audience, so always keep this in mind when you are putting items together and choosing accessories. With focussed consideration of what you require, you are less likely to dress inappropriately.

Here are a few tips to help you. Think about the items you already own or need to buy as you *Research* and *Replenish*.

Using Pattern and Colour

If you're wearing more than two colours, connect and anchor the colours together. Using accessories is the easiest way to do this, by wearing shoes and a bag or belt in the same colour, which pulls the whole outfit together with a common thread. For example, if you have a cream jumper, navy trousers, and a camel jacket, red shoes and a red bag or belt will pull it all together.

Use an item with a pattern that features a few different colours, including the colours of the items you need to tie together. Coloured and patterned scarfs and necklaces are great for this.

Look out for prints that include the *Key Colours* of your wardrobe (black and navy, camel and navy etc.), plus another *Accent Colour*, and you will always have an item to 'glue' your look together.

You could use also use a coloured boucle or tweed jacket for this, as they contain a number of different colours in the weave.

If you have a colour near your bottom half, e.g. your skirt or shoe, bring the eye up to your face by adding a touch of that colour higher up – in a scarf, earring, necklace, or in the case of reds, even in a lipstick.

How to Use Colour Combinations for Impact

A high contrast combination (e.g. a traditional dark suit/light blouse) is the traditional 'look' for classic business wear and, therefore, ideal for a meeting where you need to be authoritative, impactful and project gravitas. If your own colouring is light to medium, you'll want to wear dark-coloured suits for maximum contrast. However, if you have dark colouring, try wearing ivory or cream suits, dresses and jackets to create the same contrast, and therefore, impact.

Low contrast *Neutral Colours* (those of a similar level of light or dark) are quieter, subtler and softer. If you wear neutrals and low contrast combinations, you'll appear less visible to others and have less perceived 'power' than if you wear high contrasting tones. Therefore, if it is a general office day of perhaps low-key meetings with team members where you want to appear approachable, wear a softer or low contrast look.

For example, if you have fair colouring (blonde hair, pale skin) and a *Key Colour* is black, it is likely that white will be too harsh as a *Neutral Colour*, as this 'high contrast' combination creates a very strong, highly authoritative look. Choosing *Neutral Colours*, such as camel with ivory or sand instead, will reduce the level of contrast. However, if you often find that you are not taken seriously enough, seen as younger than you are, or perceived as 'sweet', that high contrast combination will project the authority you require.

Mixing Fabrics and Textures

Mix the fabrics but use shades of the same colour to create an effortless, harmonious and elegant look that looks understated but interesting. You can mix lightweight and heavy fabrics, wearing a silk shirt with a wool skirt, for example; but linen, even in a dark business colour, does not mix with wools and should only be worn in summer or in warm climates. If you have textured hair, tweeds and textured surface fabrics and knits will naturally suit you well.

Accessories

Any accessory must add to or support you and your outfit, either in a practical way, such as a bag to put your belongings in, or enhance you, like a belt to create a shape or necklace to fill in an open neckline and bring attention to your face.

I'VE ALWAYS THOUGHT OF ACCESSORIES
AS THE EXCLAMATION POINT OF
A WOMAN'S OUTFIT.

MICHAEL KORS

When it comes to accessories, less is more. After putting on your accessories, look in the mirror and go over your look. Check whether everything works. If something has no place being there, then take it off.

Having a relationship between all your accessories and the outfit, even if it's very subtle, is what makes you look put together, rather than someone who has randomly put on a number of disconnected pieces. For example, if you wear a multi-coloured scarf, pair it with a simple belt, shoes, earring or a bangle that picks out one of the colours in it.

Having your accessory *Core Pieces* (shoes, bag and belt) in neutral tones is vital if you want to achieve a put together look and be able to get dressed easily. Wearing shoes in a similar colour to your hair helps you to be viewed from top-to-toe. The viewer's eye will move up your body from the shoe to the hair via a belt or bag, or bracelet or necklace, to the top of your head. Even if it's done subconsciously, they will see a balance and know that your outfit has been well thought-out.

Use your body frame size to guide your choice of accessories, jewellery and prints. For example, if you are large framed then bold, chunky jewellery, large straps on bags, chunky heeled shoes and large prints are more flattering. If you have fine features or a petite frame, lighter weight fabrics, thin-heeled shoes, narrow straps on bags and delicate jewellery will complement you best.

Jewellery

When selecting a necklace, ensure the colour, style and shape relates to the outfit and either hangs well below or sits above a neckline of the dress or top.

When wearing jewellery, only have one dominant piece. It should not fight for attention with something else, so either the earrings or the necklace need to be the centre of attention, never both.

All other accessories need to support that piece and relate to it, either in style, shape, texture, line, or colour. For example, if you want the focus to be a statement necklace with a lot of detail, wear it with small, simple stud earrings.

Watches

You need to have more than one watch or watch strap. Have one in gold or silver, whichever is your preference, or a neutral leather from your *Key* or *Neutral* palette – black, tan, nude, etc. – before you buy it in any *Accent Colours*.

Spectacles and Sunglasses

If you wear spectacles, have a minimum of two pairs. Make sure you have an everyday pair in a neutral, metallic, clear, brown or tortoiseshell first before buying a pair in another colour. When buying coloured framed spectacles, always make sure the colour relates to your *Key* or *Neutral Colours* or is in an *Accent Colour* that you wear regularly.

Steer clear of patterns and colour mixes as they are distracting. Unless you want to become known for your interesting glasses, keep them modern but classic, in a shape that flatters your face shape and features. If you are in a creative field, you can opt for a more fashion-forward style.

If they are clearly branded, choose a brand that supports your status and sends the right impression. Glasses shapes and styles can date you, so try new styles every three years. There are now a number of new specialist glasses brands that are inexpensive, and will keep you looking up to date.

And it's the same with sunglasses; never wear sports or wrap-around sunglasses with business wear. As with spectacles, ensure you have an up-to-date basic frame before buying a coloured or overly embellished frame.

4.8 CREATE OUTFITS

Now you can try this out with your existing wardrobe to help you discover what you need to complete or maximise your current outfits.

- Go to your wardrobe and have a go at creating outfits, using each of your signature style formulas, one at a time.

- Start with a bottom piece (skirt or trousers) and create looks with 3-5 different tops. Also experiment with changing the jacket, shoes, jewellery, etc.

- Try each outfit on in front of mirror and take a photo of the ones that work the best.

- Look at your notes from *Review* to remind yourself of your personal colouring and contrast level. Try creating 'high contrast' and 'low contrast' combinations, so you can see the difference in impact, the *Qualities* that each outfit projects, and what suits you.

- Make a photo folder on your smartphone so you can find them all in one place. If you take pictures on your tablet, you can write directly on the image, and put a note where an alternative item can be used.

- ONCE YOU'VE TRIED THE FIRST COMBINATION ON THAT REALLY WORKS, YOU CAN TRY FURTHER VARIATIONS, WITH ANOTHER SHOE OR COLOURED TOP, FOR EXAMPLE, AS A 'FLAT LAY' – LAYING OUT THE ITEMS AS A GROUP SO YOU CAN SEE EVERYTHING IN THE OUTFIT, RATHER THAN TAKING A PICTURE OF YOU WEARING THEM.

- WHEN YOU HAVE 3-5 OUTFITS IN ONE FORMULA, MOVE ON TO THE NEXT FORMULA AND DO THE SAME.

- TRY USING A PATTERNED ITEM TO PULL TOGETHER AN OUTFIT. IF YOU DON'T YET OWN ANYTHING WITH A FEW DIFFERENT COLOURS IN IT, PUT IT ON YOUR LIST TO LOOK FOR WHEN YOU START YOUR *RESEARCH*.

- WHEN YOU FIND AN OUTFIT DOESN'T WORK, ASK YOURSELF WHY. WHAT IS MISSING? SOMETIMES, STYLE DETAILS JUST DON'T WORK TOGETHER, SO KEEP TRYING A FEW DIFFERENT OPTIONS. IF THE REQUIRED ITEM THAT WOULD MAKE IT WORK IS MISSING, MAKE A NOTE ON YOUR SHOPPING LIST AND TAKE A PICTURE OF THE REST OF THE OUTFIT TO REMIND YOU EXACTLY WHAT IS NEEDED TO COMPLETE THE LOOK.

- LOOK OUT FOR THE ITEMS YOU WEAR A LOT AND THAT APPEAR IN LOTS OF OUTFIT COMBINATIONS, E.G. IVORY SILK VESTS AND T-SHIRTS, WHICH ARE ESSENTIAL UNDER SUITS AND COLLARLESS JACKETS, OR NUDE LEATHER HEELS, BLACK BALLET FLATS. ONCE YOU KNOW WHICH ITEMS WILL GET HEAVY USAGE, MAKE SURE YOU HAVE MORE THAN ONE OF THEM.

STEP 4 RECAP

You should now have:

- Researched your *Neutral*, *Key* and *Accent Colours*

- Considered how to project your *Qualities*

- Looked at your wardrobe requirements

- Created some *Signature Style* formulas

- Listed your *Core* and *Character Pieces*

- Upgraded your underwear (if needed)

- Created outfits using your formulas

Now that you have considered what you actually need and will be useful for you, it's time to start your *Research*.

STEP 5 – RESEARCH

Before we begin the *Research*, remind yourself of your *Style Words* and top five *Qualities*, and look again at your *Inspiration Board* and Pinterest boards. As with most important projects, success lies in the planning, and the time you spend now on your pre-shopping *Research* will reduce the amount of time you will waste later, wandering around the shops aimlessly or trying things that are not right for you and getting disheartened.

Gaining an overview of the stores, including what is available that matches your personal style and is within your budget, enables you to start making great choices before you actually go shopping.

> **"**
>
> GIVE ME SIX HOURS TO CHOP DOWN A TREE
>
> AND I WILL SPEND THE FIRST FOUR
>
> SHARPENING THE AXE.
>
> **"**
>
> **ABRAHAM LINCOLN**

Know Your Budget

Before you start looking at clothes, you need to know what your budget is to determine the price point you will shop at.

Having a budget reminds you to be conscious about what you are spending, gives you parameters, and will help you to curb any tendencies you may have towards compulsive buying or wasting money.

Many women just don't value themselves enough to spend money on themselves. I regularly have clients that earn high salaries, live in gorgeous houses, privately educate their children and drive luxury cars who previously only shopped at Next and Zara. They will pay for luxuries for their family without a second thought, but still dress themselves in cheap, low quality clothes that should only be worn by someone starting out in their career. They don't invest in good quality clothes, because deep down, they don't think they are worth it.

If you owned a lot of cheap clothes that ended up in the charity shop bin bags during your clear out, it should be a wake-up call. My motto is *'buy less and buy best'*; one great dress or suit is *always* better than two cheap ones. On the other hand, if you have previously underinvested or found it difficult to spend money on yourself, having a budget gives you a spending goal and permission, if needed.

BUY LESS, CHOOSE WELL,

MAKE IT LAST.

VIVIENNE WESTWOOD

What you decide to invest will ultimately depend on how important this change is, and how badly you want to achieve your goal. Remember, if you buy wisely and shop intentionally, this will be an investment, not a spending spree. You may find you actually save money as everything you buy will actually be useful and get worn, which wasn't the case with your previous, haphazard approach.

If your goal is to get a promotion or new job, which inevitably comes with a salary increase, consider what achieving that goal would be worth financially. Ask yourself honestly, can you afford not to invest in your wardrobe? Is it worth a short-term investment of savings, or doing without a holiday, to get you there?

This is a good time to remind yourself that your new wardrobe will reduce your stress levels, make you feel good, give you confidence and open doors for you. When all is said and done, the image you project with your appearance means that you either look like a leader or you don't.

CLIENT STORY

SIMONE E

Assistant Head Teacher & Education Consultant

CATALYST FOR WARDROBE UPGRADE

Returning to work after maternity leave

Returning from maternity leave after my second child, I was wearing the same clothes for the school run, weekends and work. My focus was all on my kids and career, and I realised I had stopped taking care of myself and lost sense of who I was.

I no longer worked in the classroom and my role entailed speaking in front of large groups of parents, colleagues and other professionals, but my image hadn't progressed since my student days. When people met me, they thought I was younger and, therefore, less experienced and not as professional, because of the way I dressed.

Although I earned a decent wage, I'd felt I couldn't justify spending money on myself, so I bought cheap, 'disposable' items from high street shops, wearing them for a couple of months before replacing them. The clothes were ill fitting, and I never felt good. I was wasting money and increasingly felt that my clothes didn't feel like 'me'. I knew my image was negatively impacting what others thought of me at work, which affected my self-confidence, and so decided I had to do something about it.

Taking time out to go through this process helped me to reconnect with myself and what I want to achieve, and reminded me of who I am. I felt inspired again after creating the Inspiration and Pinterest boards, thinking about items I love, as well as writing down my goals and what's important to me.

Going through my entire wardrobe helped me see where I was going wrong, and what was required to get back on track. Shopping was now focussed but fun, and I discovered my new staple shops and brands. I immediately received comments from colleagues and friends about my increased confidence, and that I looked more stylish.

The clarity I now have saves me time and money, as I only shop when looking for a particular item. I look in shops I wouldn't have before, and try things with confidence. Having an organised wardrobe saves me time in the morning, and using matching hangers enables me to stay organised with very little effort

Finding my style, and having good quality clothes that I enjoy wearing, and feel like me, gives me such happiness and confidence. I would encourage every woman to take time to work on their wardrobe, as it has had such a positive impact.

5.1 WHAT'S YOUR BUDGET?

It is not possible for me to tell you how much you should spend on clothes, but a rule of thumb is an annual investment of 5% of your net annual salary. However, this is going to be different for everyone, as personal circumstances will dictate how much of your income is disposable.

Work out how much you will have to invest in a new wardrobe by considering the following:

- CALCULATE 5% OF YOUR NET ANNUAL SALARY AND DIVIDE BY 12.

- IS THAT APPROXIMATELY WHAT YOU CURRENTLY SPEND PER MONTH ON CLOTHES? DO YOU UNDERINVEST, OR DO YOU OVERSPEND?

- IF YOU ARE LOOKING FOR A PROMOTION OR A NEW JOB, WILL YOUR ANNUAL SALARY INCREASE?

- CONSIDER CURRENT SPENDING YOU COULD CUT BACK ON, IF YOU NEED TO, SUCH AS HOLIDAYS, EATING OUT, CARS, INTERIOR DESIGNERS, GARDENERS, OR PERSONAL TRAINERS.

- WHAT COULD YOU WITHDRAW FROM SAVINGS TO INVEST?

- FINALLY, WRITE DOWN YOUR BUDGET FOR INVESTING IN YOUR NEW WARDROBE.

Know Your Brands

Every clothing brand has its ideal target customer, be that a 23-year-old student, to a 45-year-old high net worth businesswomen, but unless you look into the brand carefully, it's not often clear. Knowing which brands suit your own personal style, lifestyle and taste helps to minimise your options and choices.

Finding a few brands you love saves you from wasting time in shops that are unlikely to have anything suitable. When shopping in a department store, you can avoid whole sections of the shop floor by knowing which of the hundreds of brands you like. What can look to be an overwhelming amount of choice at first glance, will suddenly appear manageable.

Below are the business style brands I most often look to when researching and shopping for a client, and they are a good starting point, regardless of your personal style tastes.

Recommended Brands

High Street

& OTHER STORIES   MANGO   MASSIMO DUTTI

TOP SHOP   UNIQLO   ZARA

Quality High Street

COS   HOBBS   JIGSAW

LIBBY LONDON   LK BENNETT   REISS

WINSER LONDON   WHISTLES

Quality Brands

ARMANI   BOSS   CEFINN

CLUB MONACO   DVF   GERARD DAREL

GOAT   J.CREW   JOSEPH

MARELLA   MARINA RINALDI   MAX MARA

PAUL SMITH   PIAZZA SEMPIONE   ROLAND MOURET

THE FOLD   THEORY   VINCE

Once you have decided how much you have to invest in your new wardrobe, and an idea of which items you need and in what quantities, you will be clearer on what price point makes sense for you. You may aspire to buy higher quality brands in the long term, but at this stage, you are likely to require more items in one go, so you may need to mix it up to stretch your budget further.

It may be a combination; for example, with most of the *Core Pieces* from quality high street brands, with the occasional piece from a high quality brand.

To give you an illustration of the wide range of prices, here is an example of the cost of a silk shirt and a pair of smart trouser across the three different price points.

Silk Blouse

- H&M/Mango/Zara £40-70

- Whistles/Reiss/L K Bennett £130-190

- Joseph/Max Mara/Theory £200/350

Smart Pair of Trousers

- H&M/Mango/Zara £20-40

- WHISTLES/REISS/L K BENNETT £110-160

- JOSEPH/MAX MARA/THEORY £200-450

5.2 WHAT'S YOUR PRICE POINT?

- FOR AN *APPROXIMATE* CALCULATION THAT WILL ESTABLISH THE AMOUNT YOU HAVE TO SPEND ON A *CORE PIECE* AND, THEREFORE, THE PRICE POINT AT WHICH YOU ARE GOING TO SHOP, DIVIDE YOUR TOTAL BUDGET BY THE NUMBER OF ITEMS YOU NEED TO BUY TO REBUILD YOUR WARDROBE. SO IF YOUR BUDGET IS £2,000 AND YOU NEED 20 PIECES, YOUR PRICE POINT IS APPROXIMATELY £100 PER ITEM, WHICH WOULD PUT YOU IN THE *QUALITY HIGH STREET* PRICE POINT.

- LIST THE SHOPS AND BRANDS THAT ARE RECOMMENDED FOR YOUR PRICE POINT, AND START THERE.

This is a rough guide only, but will help you to be realistic and enable you to readjust your expectations or your budget, if necessary.

What is Your Clothes Size in Different Brands?

Many clothing brands are international, so it's not enough just to know that you are, for example, a UK Size 12. Knowing where the brand originates makes it easier to select your right size before you even go into a changing room. European sizes are different, depending on the country, so UK Size 12 is 38 in COS (Scandinavian), 40 in Zara (Spanish) and Sandro (French) or 44 in Max Mara (Italian).

As every brand fits slightly different and uses a different measurement, it's worth investigating the measurements that are used for the sizing of any brands that are new to you, so you can get the right size first time.

For example, below are some different UK Size 12 measurements (in centimetres).

	Bust	Waist	Hips	Size
Boss	93	75	101	large
L K Bennett	91.5	73.5	100	medium
Topshop	92	74.2	98.5	medium
Sandro	92	76	104	large

5.3 CHECK YOUR INTERNATIONAL CLOTHES SIZES

- START A NEW NOTE CALLED *SIZES*.

- LOOK BACK AT THE MEASUREMENTS THAT YOU TOOK IN THE *REFLECT* STEP. WHEN YOU ARE DOING YOUR UPCOMING ONLINE RESEARCH, MAKE A NOTE OF THE SIZES ACCORDING TO YOUR MEASUREMENTS AND THE BRAND'S SIZING INFORMATION.

- SAVE A PHOTO ON YOUR SMARTPHONE OF THE INTERNATIONAL CHART FOR FUTURE EASY REFERENCE.

International Size Chart

S-M-L	USA	UK/AU/NZ	ITALY	FRANCE	GERMANY	JAPAN	RUSSIA
S	2	6	38	34	32	7	40
S	4	8	40	36	34	9	42
M	6	10	42	38	36	11	44
M	8	12	44	40	38	13	46
L	10	14	46	42	40	15	48
L	12	16	48	44	42	17	50
XL/1X	14	18	50	46	44	19	52

Online Research

Now you have a good idea of what you need to buy and your price range, you are ready to actually start browsing online. Researching online before stepping foot in a shop will help you to find the brands that resonate with you and suit your personal style, which means you'll spend less time needlessly browsing in stores.

If you are not very interested in clothes, it's even more important to look online at what is currently available, as you are likely to feel out of touch. If you didn't even recognise many of the names of the brands and stores I recommended, this step is vital.

By visiting a brand's website and seeing how they present their clothes, you'll be able to get a feel for the customer they are aiming for. From the look of the model to the style of photos, colours and fonts used in the branding, you can begin to see the difference between brands at your price point. You will see photos or even a video of the clothes on a model. Even if that is not your size, it gives a better idea of the style and shape of a garment than when you see it on a hanger.

Researching online also gives an overview of what the current looks are, so you can compare different brands' looks against each other. When you finally enter a store that you have already visited online, it will feel familiar and you'll feel more confident and less overwhelmed.

5.4 RESEARCH BRANDS ONLINE

Before you step foot in a shop, I want you to look at the websites of my recommended brands list. This is not a definitive list, but these are the brands I suggest you look at to start with.

- REFER BACK TO YOUR NOTES, SHOPPING LIST AND THE ITEMS YOU LIKED ON PINTEREST BEFORE, AND REMAIN TOTALLY FOCUSSED. *THESE ARE THE ONLY THINGS YOU SHOULD BE LOOKING AT.* DON'T GET DISTRACTED BY LOOKING AT KIDS' CLOTHES OR BEACH COVER-UPS!

- KEEP YOUR LIST OF *QUALITIES* AND *STYLE WORDS* IN FRONT OF YOU AS YOU BROWSE TO MAKE SURE THAT WHATEVER YOU ARE SHOPPING FOR REFLECTS THEM.

- USE A DESKTOP OR LAPTOP COMPUTER IF POSSIBLE (RATHER THAN A PHONE OR TABLET) AND VISIT THE WEBSITES OF THE BRANDS IN YOUR RECOMMENDED PRICE POINT FIRST BEFORE VISITING OTHERS, TO GET A REALISTIC SENSE OF WHAT IS OUT THERE FOR YOU.

- DOWNLOAD THE PINTEREST 'PIN BUTTON' TO YOUR BROWSER (THERE ARE INSTRUCTIONS OF HOW TO DO THIS IN THE 'HELP CENTRE' IN PINTEREST) SO YOU CAN PIN DIRECTLY FROM RETAILER WEBSITES.

- CREATE PINTEREST BOARDS TO SAVE PINS OF THE ITEMS YOU FIND. YOU CAN HAVE A BOARD FOR EACH GARMENT CATEGORY, E.G. 'WINTER COATS TO TRY ON', OR A GENERIC 'WORKWEAR' BOARD.

- CLICK ON THE 'PENCIL' ICON TO ADD A NOTE TO EACH PIN. INCLUDE THE BRAND NAME, PRICE, SEASON AND YEAR, I.E. L K BENNETT £89 SS19, SO YOU CAN KEEP TRACK OF THEM AT A GLANCE.

- MAKE A NOTE OF ITEMS YOU FIND THAT YOU LIKE AND WANT TO TRY ON IN THE STORES.

- TAKE A SCREEN GRAB OF ANY ITEMS THAT YOU LIKE BUT ARE UNABLE TO PIN.

Pre-Shopping Preparation

Now that you have done your online research, you are ready to go on a pre-shopping trip. A day or two before a shopping session, I will spend a couple of hours minimum browsing the stores I feel are right for my client. This allows me to see who has what, and also spot other items I would like her to try. Once I have an overview of what is available, I can then create a plan for shopping.

> ❝
>
> BY FAILING TO PREPARE,
>
> YOU ARE PREPARING TO FAIL.
>
> **BENJAMIN FRANKLIN**
>
> ❞

I know you may feel you don't have the time for one shopping trip, let alone two, especially if you hate shopping, but it is worth it. A couple of hours spent browsing and comparing items from one brand to another can be eye opening, especially if you have never shopped in a considered way before, and it means you avoid wasting money on mistaken purchases.

5.5 UNDERTAKE IN-STORE RESEARCH

- GET YOUR DIARY OUT AND SET A FEW HOURS ASIDE TO UNDERTAKE A BROWSING TRIP.

- BEFORE YOU GO, DOWNLOAD THE PINTEREST APP TO YOUR SMARTPHONE, SO YOU CAN EASILY VIEW YOUR STYLE ASPIRATIONS AND ANY SPECIFIC ITEMS YOU LIKED THE LOOK OF WHEN BROWSING ONLINE STORES.

- HAVE ALL YOUR NOTES AND SHOPPING LIST TO HAND.

- VISIT YOUR PREFERRED BRANDS TO GAIN AN OVERVIEW OF WHO HAS WHAT, BEFORE YOU START BUYING.

- GET UP CLOSE TO ANY ITEMS YOU SAW ONLINE, AND FEEL THE FABRIC, PARTICULARLY THE HIGH STREET BRANDS, WHICH OFTEN LOOK BETTER IN PHOTOS THAN THEY ARE IN REALITY.

If you plan to shop in a city that is not near where you live, and you are unable to do a separate browsing session before shopping, I recommend you start your shopping day with at least an hour or two of browsing.

STEP 5 RECAP

You should now have:

- CALCULATED YOUR BUDGET

- WORKED OUT WHICH BRANDS WILL MEET YOUR NEEDS

- SET YOUR PRICE-POINT

- CHECKED YOUR INTERNATIONAL SIZE EQUIVALENT

- CONDUCTED ONLINE RESEARCH AND FOUND SOME PREFERRED BRANDS

- BEEN ON A PRE-SHOPPING RESEARCH TRIP

You are now ready for the big moment – your first proper shopping trip to *Replenish* your wardrobe.

STEP 6 – REPLENISH

In this chapter, we start to *Replenish* your wardrobe. Contrary to popular opinion, many women do not like shopping. In fact, most of my clients tell me they hate it. So I really want to prepare and support you so that you can have a pleasant and worthwhile experience, and I am going to give you some tips on how to shop and what to look for, so shopping will be much easier, and hopefully enjoyable!

Having gone through the previous steps, you have given yourself a head start. You know your budget, the price point and brands to head for. You have your list of *Qualities* and *Style Words* to keep you on track, and know where the gaps are in your wardrobe and any particular items required. You also have some idea of the colour palette you'd like to try, your accurate measurements, and your signature style formulas to create your preferred look.

When to Shop

Go early in the day, and on a weekday if possible. The shops are completely different mid-week to weekends. I never shop at a weekend with a client, as it's just too crowded to do what we need, and time is wasted in the queues for dressing rooms and tills.

Just as the money you are spending is an investment in your career, so is the time. If you were actively seeking a promotion or interviewing for a new role, you would invest hours of your time in preparation. I urge you to take shopping for new items just as seriously, and invest the time that is needed to get the result you require. Take a day of annual leave, or put childcare in place to allow you time on a weekday. Don't shop with kids in tow. You need to be either on your own, or have a friend who is solely there to assist you with getting sizes and giving feedback. If you cannot go shopping on a weekday, and are not prepared to take time off work, then upgrading your business image is obviously not that important to you.

If you must shop on the weekend, it's advisable to go as

soon as the stores open. The difference between the morning and afternoon is like night and day, so the earlier the better. Sundays are often less crowded than Saturdays, and the shops have the half-hour browsing time, so you can get in there even earlier. Also, you can often park on city centre streets nearer the shops, even in London's West End, which saves you carrying your purchases around.

At this stage of the process, please don't try to squeeze shopping in after work. Long term, once you have your wardrobe up and running, after work is likely to be the time you can regularly get a couple of hours shopping in. This is fine when you are just looking for additional pieces, but at this stage, it isn't advisable.

Before You Go

There are a few additional things you can do to prepare, so as to give yourself the best chance of success. These may seem blindingly obvious, but it is amazing how many people don't consider the little things that contribute towards a positive experience.

Plan to Enjoy it

Unfortunately, what you think and feel about shopping will shape your experience of it. If you head out thinking, "I hate shopping",

"I never find anything", "It's too busy", "I'm bound to come home empty handed", you will only feel defeated before you've started.

> **❝**
>
> ENTHUSIASM IS THE MOTHER OF EFFORT,
>
> AND WITHOUT IT NOTHING GREAT
>
> WAS EVER ACHIEVED.
>
> **❞**
>
> **RALPH WALDO EMERSON**

Even if that has been your experience before now, it doesn't have to be this time, so wipe the slate clean of any negative past experiences. Please don't view it as something you have to get out of the way; instead, go with time to spare and the intention of enjoying yourself. It's a chance for you to be creative, experiment, and more importantly, to have fun!

Dress Sensibly

The more you're prepared, the more you can enjoy yourself!

I am constantly amazed by what people turn up for a shopping trip wearing or carrying.

When I contact a client with final arrangements, you might think we were going hiking, not shopping. I often say, *"Bring a bottle of water and a snack, travel light and wear comfortable shoes."*

Shopping is an expedition of sorts. It is dehydrating being in stores for a while, and also tiring. So, just as when you are preparing for a hiking trip, make sure that you dress appropriately and have all the right gear.

You will be in and out of changing rooms, so wear items without too many buttons, preferably a neutral coloured or white t-shirt, and trousers that can be taken on and off easily. Wear your best, seam-free underwear, and avoid dresses, as you won't have a top to wear when you try on trousers. Wear shoes or boots that are easy to pull on and off without the need to undo and tie laces. Even in winter, don't wear a heavy coat, as once you get in the shops, you will be hot and uncomfortable. Carry as little as possible and use an across-body bag so your hands are free.

Hopefully, you will have got the message that this first shopping trip is not to be squeezed in after work, or while on the way to somewhere else. You will have planned the trip, so there is no need to have a big bag with paperwork, a laptop or a gym kit with you.

How to Choose Clothes

Here are some final tips so you can shop efficiently, and a few things I feel are worth repeating and to look out for when shopping.

Quality, not Quantity

I hear from many of my clients that when you are unsure of what works, you may often shop in cheaper stores because if you make a mistake and don't wear the item, you won't have wasted much money.

However, to look like a leader and display executive presence, you will need to focus on buying good quality clothes. Whatever industry you are in, whatever style you prefer and whatever dress code there is, wearing quality clothes will give gravitas to your look.

Studies show that quality counts in business, and that wearing a made-to-measure suit, rather than an off-the-peg equivalent, will positively affect the judgments people make in those crucial first three seconds[14]. In a study where the same men wore a high street suit and a tailor-made suit, people judged the wearer of the better quality suit to be more confident, successful, flexible and a higher earner.

Some of the cheaper high street brands do offer high quality fabrics and well-made items, but they are not obvious in store and are often mingled in with other stock. It's worth looking online to see what is available in the premium range, then when you go in the store, you will know exactly what you are going in there for.

For example, in H&M, look for the 'Premium Quality' range, Mango has 'Premium' and 'Committed' ranges, and 'Zara Woman' provides better quality than their 'Basics' range. In Topshop, look for the cream and black card swing tags from the 'Exclusive Collection' pieces, which are made of quality fabrics, as well as being better designed and made.

Fabric

The reason that designer clothes look and feel so good is due to the quality of the cloth and the attention given to the garment's construction. This is why one of the most important considerations when assessing a garment is the fabric and lining. When people manage to make high street buys look like designer items, it's usually down to the fabric, and vice versa. If it looks cheap, you will look cheap and not like an authoritative leader. In particular, always check the lining of jackets and dresses, as this is often next to your skin, and if it's a low quality manmade fabric, you will be uncomfortable and sweaty and not *feel* good, whatever it looks like.

Look out for natural fibre fabrics as much as possible or mixes, combining them with viscose, elastane or other manmade fibres that offer flexibility.

Colour

Shopping and trying on new garments is a good time to experiment to see which of the colours that you may not have tried before suit you, and it's time to try out the colours you are considering as your *Key, Neutral and Accent Colours*. Unfortunately, a changing room with natural light is almost unheard of. Try to locate a mirror near the front of the store, or where there is natural light, and hold a few different coloured items up at your face to see how things suit you in the daylight. Also, assess if the colour will blend in with or enhance your colour palette, and if it will be easy to mix and match it with the items you already own.

Suitability

The upkeep of a garment needs consideration too, so it doesn't end up unworn, or mistakenly destroyed in an accidental wash. If you occupy a senior role, I would expect quite a number of the items in your wardrobe to be dry-clean only, but make sure you balance garment upkeep requirements with your lifestyle.

Some simple 'dry clean' items can be gently machine washed, but before buying any item of clothing, always check the washing instructions to see if it's going to be too much of a hassle and not worth the additional cost and bother.

How to Shop

These practical tips will make your shopping trip feel less overwhelming and more enjoyable.

Scan and Gather

There is a skill to shopping, and it *can* be learned. I call it '*scan and gather*'. Having a clear intention of what you are looking for gives you the ability to visually sift through the items quickly. Being focussed and clear about *exactly* what you are looking for means you will not become overwhelmed when faced with the hundreds of items that are available.

6.1 SHOP USING THE 'SCAN AND GATHER' TECHNIQUE

Now it's time for action. You should be ready to hit the shops.

- HEAD TO THE STORES AND BRANDS HIGHLIGHTED IN YOUR RESEARCH, AND IGNORE THOSE THAT ARE NOT SUITED TO YOUR SIGNATURE STYLE OR TASTE. START WITH ONE OR TWO, MAXIMUM THREE, ITEM CATEGORIES FROM YOUR LIST, FOR EXAMPLE, 'WORK DRESSES AND WHITE BLOUSES', AND *ONLY* LOOK FOR THOSE.

- WHEN YOU HAVE COVERED THE STORE, OR FLOOR IF YOU ARE IN A DEPARTMENT STORE, OR IF YOU CAN'T CARRY ANY MORE ITEMS, HEAD TO THE CHANGING ROOM TO TRY ON WHAT YOU HAVE.

- USE YOUR INTUITION AND LISTEN TO YOUR GUT. IF SOMETHING DOESN'T FEEL RIGHT, DON'T BUY IT, EVEN IF YOU FEEL YOU SHOULD.

- ONCE YOU HAVE TRIED ON THESE ITEMS, ASK THE PAY DESK TO HOLD ANYTHING THAT YOU MAY WANT TO BUY LATER, AND START SCANNING AGAIN FOR ANOTHER CATEGORY.

- AND REPEAT.

Take pictures of anything you love and feel is a strong contender, and make a note of any features that work, even if the garment as a whole doesn't; for example, a great neckline, sleeve length or colour.

In time, when you are adding the odd item to your wardrobe, and once you have got good at scanning and gathering, you will be able to look for more categories at a time. However, I advise you to always shop with a list, even a mental one, and in a targeted way.

Always Try Things On

Skipping the fitting room doesn't save you time in the long run. Even if you are buying what you think is an identical item to the one you already own, it could have been made in a different factory and fit quite differently. Try at least two sizes of any garment where a good fit is of paramount importance, such as a jacket, jeans, and whenever there is any doubt in your mind. Even if you look in the mirror and think it's fine, just see what happens if you go up or down a size. It's better to spend your budget on a quality high street item that fits you perfectly than to blow your budget on an expensive piece that doesn't.

Consider Alterations

Items that are too tight, too loose, too short or long need to be altered immediately or left in the store.

Think back to your *Qualities*. If you want to look like a leader, one thing is for certain, and it's worth repeating again as it is so important – your clothes must fit well. A male senior executive would have his suit made to measure or expect it to be tailored to fit, and luckily for him, the stores he shops in will have a tailor on hand. However, the majority of women still hold a belief that clothes should fit them off the peg, and that something is wrong with their shape, not the item, when it doesn't fit.

Most stores at the level you should be shopping in at this stage in your career will undertake alterations, so ask the assistant and swallow the cost.

If you know you have 'fit issues', ask friends for recommendations of a good alterations person or tailor, then find out the prices involved, and allow for them in your budget.

CLIENT STORY

SARAH K

GLOBAL FINANCIAL COMPLIANCE MANAGER

CATALYST FOR WARDROBE UPGRADE
Confused and frustrated with her wardrobe

I was exasperated with everything to do with my wardrobe, as it wasn't giving me what I felt I needed. I was confused about how to dress for work without losing my sense of playfulness, and had no idea how or where to shop for this. As a result, I kept reinventing myself every few months, but I wanted to define my style and stick to it.

Before going through this process I had never thought about what I was wearing was communicating, or how it impacted my self-confidence. At first, when I realised certain pieces of clothes in my wardrobe were short or skimpy, I was embarrassed. But I suddenly saw how I was portraying myself, and knew that by wearing inappropriate and cheap clothes this made me look young and inexperienced, and I realised that I was not respecting myself and my body enough.

When shopping, I finally learned that my size doesn't matter; before, a size 16 pair of trousers would have felt horrifying, but when they fitted so well and made me feel amazing, I didn't care about the label anymore! It was a real turning point in the way I see myself, my body, and what I choose to wear, improving my confidence, and giving me a boost I never even realised I needed. I found styles that suited me, and bought fabulous basics from quality brands that made me look credible at work. I also had some items altered to fit me properly, which has made a huge difference to my overall look.

Just after I upgraded my wardrobe, I got a new job. When I started, the way I was dressed had a huge impact; firstly on my confidence, but also on how people perceived me. I believe it played a huge part in accelerating my career, as I was offered an international assignment for six months after only being there a few weeks. This was the most important step up I'd ever had in my career, and I was in total shock when it happened.

My newfound confidence helped me, and my image made me so credible that I was dealing with the CEO and his C-suite, day in, day out – it was just brilliant.

It's amazing how much my career has gone into overdrive. I've been in the new role for just over a year and I'm already discussing promotions with my manager.

Focus

The key to successful shopping is focus. Small chunks of focussed time will work just as well as a whole day. But I mean really focussed, no multitasking, no kids, no talking on the phone as you browse or try on. Remember, only look for 1-3 items at a time from your priority list. To start, treat your *Core Pieces* as the priority, but note and photograph any *Character Pieces* that will bring interest and complete outfits too, and buy them once you have enough of the former to create at least three different looks.

You will have to try on lots of clothes – there is no escaping it – but please don't get disheartened when trying them on. The reason you have gaps in your wardrobe is probably because those missing items are harder for you to find. Trousers are particularly troublesome, as it is almost impossible to guess the fit from the hanger, so it is trial and error.

Just keep going! I want you to try things you may never have considered before and, therefore, you will have a lot of *no's* before you find a *yes*.

Ask for Help

Unfortunately, many stores are severely lacking in good one-to-one customer service. Always make sure you ask the shop assistant to fetch another size, and to check the stock room if you can't see the size you need on the shop floor.

Sometimes, sales staff do have time to offer personal service and can be very helpful, particularly midweek and in smaller stores, or brand concessions within a department store. Increasingly, brands are investing in staff training, and as a result, you may be helped by a brilliant salesperson. This can especially be an issue in small, owner-run boutiques, who may well tell you whatever you need to hear to make you buy. As you have done your preparation, this shouldn't be a problem. Hold firm and don't be influenced if your gut tells you it's not right for you or what you were looking for. Thankfully, there is most often a middle ground; there are some fantastic sales staff and boutique owners who will take on the role of your personal stylist and can be a wonderful help, or a fitting room assistant who will fetch you different sizes, and suggest other styles that would fit or suit you better.

Take a Break

Make sure you have a break and a cup of tea and slice of cake along the way. Don't feel you have to put your head down and get on with it like a chore. Ideally, you will be able to get a good number of items to *Replenish* your wardrobe in one session, but take it as it comes and don't get defeated if it takes time and a number of trips.

If you start to criticise yourself or your size or shape, instead of the clothes, the shop gets crowded, you become grumpy and tired, or the music is making your ears bleed, just quit and go back another day, or switch to the next item on your priority list and come back to it another time.

6.2 FINAL CHECKS

You have chosen a garment, the fabric is great, it fits, you like the style and the colour suits you.

Before you head to the pay desk, check:

- WHAT IS IT USEFUL FOR?

- WHERE WILL YOU WEAR IT?

- WHAT WORDS WOULD YOU USE TO DESCRIBE IT?

- IS IT ALIGNED WITH YOUR *STYLE WORDS* OR *QUALITIES* YOU ARE LOOKING TO PROJECT, AS DISCOVERED IN THE *REFLECT* STEP?

- DOES IT FIT WITH YOUR SIGNATURE STYLE, AND ADD SOMETHING NEW TO YOUR WARDROBE? IT MUST IMPROVE AN OUTFIT OR ADD TO THE FUNCTIONALITY OF YOUR WARDROBE AND FULFIL A REQUIREMENT.

- YOU KNOW OF THREE ITEMS IN YOUR WARDROBE IT WILL BE WORN WITH (YOU NEED TO COME UP WITH AT LEAST THREE).

When you are in the process of building your wardrobe up, you may not yet own the three things it will require, but they should be *Core Pieces* that are already on your priority list.

Beyond Your Shopping Trip

Online Shopping

Although I don't advocate it, I know you will probably shop online at some point, so here are some online shopping rules.

- DON'T BROWSE AIMLESSLY TO PASS THE TIME, E.G. ON A COMMUTE OR WHILE WATCHING TV. ALWAYS HAVE A LIST AND SHOP INTENTIONALLY FOR SPECIFIC ITEMS ONLY.

- HOWEVER, IF YOU DO BROWSE, DON'T ADD ITEMS TO YOUR BASKET. INSTEAD, ADD ITEMS YOU LIKE TO PINTEREST TO REVISIT THEM WHEN YOU CAN GIVE YOUR PURCHASE CONSIDERATION AND CHECK IT IS REALLY WHAT YOU NEED.

- Don't sign up for brand emails, and once you have bought something online, unsubscribe ASAP. They will advertise to you whenever you are online, email you relentlessly, tempt you with offers and tease you with the latest looks. You don't need this. You choose when you need something and control when you want to shop.

Sales and Discount Clothing Stores

I love a bargain as much as the next person, but sales and huge stores of reduced old season stock are dangerous, so proceed with caution. Discounts are great when there is a quality brand or item that you love but it is outside your price range. This is where *Research* pays dividends as you can stalk a more expensive brand, and be ready to pounce when an item comes on sale. However, many of the great pieces will never make it to the sale rail, and the items that do are usually there for a reason; the fit's a bit odd, the neckline does not sit quite right, or it's got just a bit too much going on.

This is where you must apply the shopping rules I've mentioned already:

- Stay focussed.

- Shop with a list.

- CHECK IT FITS YOUR SIGNATURE STYLE.

- IT WORKS WITH YOUR EXISTING COLOUR PALETTE.

- YOU CAN THINK OF THREE ITEMS YOU CAN WEAR IT WITH.

Always check the returns policy, so if it doesn't work with your other items, as you imagined, you can return it. If you can't make it work with what you own, and need to buy other pieces to make it useable, it is costing you money and so it is a false economy.

When You Get Home

After the trip, you should have a few bags of great, new items that are going to be fantastic pieces for your work wardrobe. Now the task is to work out what goes together with what, and put some go-to outfits together using the signature style formulas you worked on in Step 5.

6.3 OUTFIT BUILDING

Take a good look at all the pieces you already had, along with the new pieces you have just bought. Now you need to work out what will go together.

- UNPACK YOUR NEW ITEMS AND TRY THEM ON AGAIN IN FRONT OF THE MIRROR.

- CREATE A MINIMUM OF THREE FULL OUTFITS USING YOUR EXISTING WARDROBE WITH THE NEW ITEMS BOUGHT ON THE SAME OR RECENT SHOPPING TRIPS.

- TAKE PHOTOS, AND MAKE A NOTE OF ANYTHING THAT YOU STILL NEED.

- IF YOU CAN'T MAKE ANY OF YOUR NEW PURCHASES WORK, FOR WHATEVER REASON, RETURN THEM AS SOON AS POSSIBLE.

STEP 6 RECAP

You should now have:

- PREPARED WELL FOR YOUR SHOPPING TRIP

- EXECUTED A SHOPPING TRIP USING THE "SCAN AND GATHER" TECHNIQUE

- CONDUCTED FINAL CHECKS BEFORE BUYING ANYTHING

- BOUGHT SOME GREAT ITEMS

- MADE OUTFITS OUT OF YOUR NEW AND EXISTING ITEMS

Congratulations on completing your first focussed shopping trip. You should now have lots of options for work outfits. Now that your clothes have been dealt with, we need to take a moment to *Refine* your image.

STEP 7 – REFINE

Your visual image and 'look' is more than just your clothes; there are other aspects of your appearance that will need consideration if you want to really look like a leader.

Being well groomed does not mean looking like a mannequin, or being photo ready. Instead, it means you look like you have made an effort with how you present yourself, are aware of your appearance, and respectful to your employer, colleagues, and clients.

Sociologists have found that women who have made more of an effort with their appearance (wear make-up, and have a blow dry and manicure) are more financially successful[15].

Andrew Penner, the joint researcher on this study, said for women, grooming was more important than looks when it came to earnings. "The economic returns aren't being given to people who have a certain kind of body, but rather to people who present their bodies in a certain kind of way," he said. "Attractiveness is not something that you have, but something that you do."

In this chapter, I highlight the different factors that contribute to a well-groomed professional appearance, and give some tips and low maintenance strategies to help you achieve this, even if you would really rather not be bothered or don't have the time.

Make-Up

Make-up is arguably the most important aspect of your grooming, as it plays a vital part in how you are perceived.

Wearing make-up is the norm for a senior executive in our culture, at this time. It shows others that you have made an effort, that you make the most of yourself, and it can give you added confidence too.

You may be someone who bemoans societal pressure to wear make-up, but I feel you are actually in an advantageous position. Yes, men are lucky that they don't have to spend those few minutes more getting ready in the morning, but the transformative power of make-up is amazing.

There are great products at your disposal to enhance what you have; concealer to cover dark circles, foundation to even out a blotchy skin tone, eyeliner to enhance and make eyes appear larger, and lipstick to add colour as it fades with age.

ALL WOMEN ARE PRETTY WITHOUT MAKE-UP

– BUT WITH THE RIGHT MAKE-UP

CAN BE PRETTY POWERFUL.

BOBBI BROWN

Once you get to your thirties, your own make-up routine will have settled in. You will know by now if you are someone who likes to paint on a fully made-up face each day, or washes her face with soap and water and wears nothing but moisturiser, or like most women, you fall somewhere in between, depending on what the day ahead holds.

Many women complain that they don't have time to put on make-up. However, it doesn't have to take more than five minutes, if that's all you have, and it really is worth it.

Leading make-up artist Florrie White has a client list of A-list film stars and celebrities, and her work regularly appears on the covers of *Vogue* and other high fashion glossy magazines.

Below are Florrie's Eight Make-Up Bag Everyday Essentials for a busy career woman. If you don't currently wear make-up, using just these few basic items will change your look, and make you look more polished.

Florrie White's Make-Up Essentials

Long Lasting Foundation and Concealer

Foundation is a very personal choice, and it is equally essential to find the right texture and finish for you and your skin type, as it is to find the correct shade. With a clean, make-up free face, get advice at the beauty counter. Try the product around your nose, cheeks and chin and check the shade in various lighting. Make sure you get a sample to try out, and wear it for a few days before you purchase to see how it feels and works on your skin.

Eyebrow Make-up

Eyebrows instantly frame your features and give a lift to the most tired of faces. There are numerous options, from a pencil to an angled brush used with a powder – it's personal choice, depending on your requirements.

Eyelash Curlers

Curling your eyelashes not only creates an illusion of longer lashes; it also lifts the lashes to allow more light into the iris, which in turn opens out the eye and gives a more wide-awake look.

Eyeshadow Pencil

Every eye colour suits warm browns, chocolates and champagne shades. A smudging of chocolate brown around the eye enhances the shape and frames the eye. This can be done more easily by using eyeshadow pencils, rather than powder shadow and a brush.

Mascara

Mascara, in either brown or black, depending on your colouring, is the absolute bare minimum and essential to every make-up routine.

Blusher or Bronzer

Warmth and a healthy glow can be added to cheeks. Use a powder blush or bronzer with a large blusher brush, sweeping the apples of the cheeks up to the temples, over the bridge of the nose and a dab on the chin.

Lipstick or Lip Balm

Find your perfect nude lipstick and also a signature red and/ or plum shade for evening, or when more colour is required. If you don't wear lipstick, invest in a tinted lip balm. Find one that incorporates skincare for anti-lines and plumpness.

Powder

Maintain a matt look throughout the day with a pressed powder compact, or a fixing spray.

Florrie's list covers the absolute minimum products that you need in your make-up bag. However, if you haven't updated your look for a while or have no idea about make-up, I advise you to book a lesson with a make-up artist that is not affiliated with any particular brand, so they can advise you on products that really are the best for you.

If you want some quick advice and to visit just one counter, my preferred brands for a professional, natural look are either Bobbi Brown, Laura Mercier or Trish McEvoy.

Hair

As with your clothes, you need a hairstyle that you can forget about and looks good 'as is', without constant readjustment. If you don't have one already, find a good hairdresser.

With age, hair becomes thinner and drier, and requires a lot more work to look good. Remember that women who have hair that looks like they have just stepped out of a salon, probably have.

The important thing about having great hair is to be honest; about your hair type, lifestyle, what suits you, and how much time and money you are prepared to spend on its maintenance. You need to think about the time that is required to get your hair looking professional. With a few compromises, there is a sweet spot, which a hairdresser you trust can help you to find.

You don't get great looking hair without effort, and just as the media sells the illusion of a perfect body, or a natural, line-free face, you are also sold the illusion of middle-aged women with amazingly lush, long hair. I know a few middle-aged women who were born with, and still have, fantastic thick, glossy hair, but they are the exception. The use of hair extensions by celebrities is prolific, so don't be tricked into thinking most long hair is natural, and an attainable benchmark to set yourself against.

If your hair is long but you mostly wear it in a ponytail or a butterfly clip at work, it's time to get it cut into a style. If it's worn up, it should look intentionally so, in an 'up style', even if it's in a 'messy bun'. It must never look like you have just whacked it up in a ponytail at the last minute before running out the door.

In recent years, the availability of blow-dry bars has boomed, especially in London and the larger cities. If you have anything longer than a very short length, a professional blow-dry can do wonders and makes a huge difference to the finish. We have all experienced that feeling of leaving the salon with a bounce and swish! It really can put a spring in your step if you have an important event. You can extend your blow dry by using a dry shampoo between washes, so it is worth considering if you have a conference or a week of important meetings ahead.

And if you *ever* go into work with wet hair, I only have one word to say. Don't.

One final hair-related issue I must mention is playing with your hair. This is regularly seen with women but it's rarely an issue for men. Constant touching and flicking of a fringe is at first distracting, and then becomes an annoyance, which relays a lack of self-awareness and confidence. Fiddling and fidgeting with your fringe, brushing back the hair that's falling in your face and tucking behind your ears is usually a totally unconscious habit, and hard to notice in yourself, but be aware of it and check how often you move it to one side or how much you touch it.

Skin Care

If you don't have a skincare and beauty routine of sorts by the time you are in your thirties, don't waste any more time. A good skincare routine, and cleansing in particular, is essential and as important as make-up. You don't have to buy the most expensive products but do spend five minutes cleansing, especially at night. Moisturising your eyes, face and neck will reap huge rewards while you sleep, and the results will be staring at you in the mirror in the morning.

The products you use have a big impact on your skin and how you age. Whether you have the budget for luxurious cream at over £100 a pot or £20 from Boots, there are now amazing products available containing anti-ageing essentials, such as retinol, hyaluronic acid, and Coenzyme Q10, among others.

Spending a bit more on beauty products usually means the ingredients are better quality; however, with newer brands, such as The Ordinary, you can find high quality ingredients at a fraction of the price of high-end beauty brands.

Teeth

One of the strongest parts of your image is your smile, and therefore, your teeth are very important. Cosmetic dentistry is becoming the norm, as people become more aware of the difference that having a nice smile can make, both to their confidence and the impression on others.

Even if you had a brace as a teenager, over time, your teeth are likely to have shifted and become crooked. Add to this the years of drinking tea, coffee, red wine and maybe smoking, which are likely to have taken their toll. Teeth whitening and straightening with invisible braces, such as Invisalign, is now so accessible and affordable that more and more people have better teeth than a decade ago. This is not about creating the fake, whiter than white Hollywood smile, but a good smile, with straight teeth can have a huge impact on your confidence and how you appear to others.

If you think there is room for improvement when it comes to your teeth, it's worth having a chat with your dentist about what could be done to improve your smile.

Nails

Your nails can make or break your overall impression. Nails with dirt underneath or bitten to the quick will be noticed and give off a less than favourable impression.

If you want to be seen as a leader, a regular manicure is recommended, even if you skip the nail polish. If you have an important meeting or presentation, I would say it is essential.

Having your nails done is much easier now, thanks to the proliferation of nail bars, and the invention of gel manicures. Gel polish is set with UV light, dries instantly, and is much tougher and longer-lasting. Investing an hour of your time on a manicure that can last two to three weeks without a chip, depending on the colour, is well worth it. Choose a quality brand such as CND Shellac – my personal favourite as it is so easily removed and therefore less damaging.

Avoid bright 'fashion' colours, such as green or yellow, as they can be distracting, but nicely painted nails in a bright red colour, or *Key Colour*, such as navy, grey or even black, can be a great way to show some individuality, yet still look highly professional. A natural shade ensures that your nails will look healthy and shiny, and last up to a month, as the regrowth is barely noticeable.

Long-Lasting Grooming

Let's be honest, there are better ways to spend your time than in front of the mirror.

Many women are extremely time poor, but realise how important looking well put together is for their career. Luckily, one area of the beauty world that has come on in leaps and bounds over the last decade is in the area of long-lasting solutions to looking good without daily effort.

There are many options available to women who are time poor or don't like the bother but want the results, from gel nail polish (mentioned previously), eyelash extensions and semi-permanent eyeliner to Keratin 'Brazilian blow-dry' treatments.

Permanent Eyeliner

If you are someone who is not into wearing make-up and/or have never spent much time practicing or applying it, getting your make-up right can be difficult. Permanent eyeliner stays put without smudging or the need to reapply – a major bonus if you work long days and want to remain looking good with no effort at all.

The mere mention of permanent eyeliner might conjure up an image of a fake, overly made-up look, but if it's applied by a good practitioner with a 'less is more' ethos, it is amazing, and a huge time saver. It's a fantastic alternative for those with sensitive eyes who find it uncomfortable to wear mascara and eye liner, or who find it hard to apply eye make-up due to unsteady hands, poor eyesight or other health issues. It is also brilliant if you swim or exercise regularly before work or in your lunch hour.

El Truchan, a permanent make-up specialist who works with a lot of women who require natural looking make-up, says, "Increasingly, my clients are time poor professionals, sports enthusiasts, or women with medical conditions, who choose the procedure over the need to apply conventional make-up."

As a guide, it lasts between one to five years before a new treatment is required, although refresher colour boosts are recommended for maintenance between 6-18 months from the original treatment.

Microblading Eyebrows

If you have over-plucked, sparse or thin eyebrows, pencilling in eyebrows everyday becomes both tedious and time-consuming, and they run the risk of smudging.

Microblading is the application of semi-permanent pigment in fine strokes that match the direction of your natural brow hairs, providing you with perfect brows, regardless of the natural growth of your brow hairs or shape, and the results last for up to a year.

It can also offer huge psychological benefit to women who have lost their eyebrows through chemotherapy or disfigurement, or who suffer from hot flushes during the menopause and wipe their brows a lot.

Eyelash Extensions

Don't be put off by the 'false eyelash' look that is so dominant among many younger women. If done well, eyelash extensions, where one or multiple very fine extensions are applied to one of your natural lashes, can look incredibly natural and create a fresh, youthful appearance. Not only can they increase your confidence, but they save you time in the mornings. You don't put mascara on, but your eyes are more defined, as the thicker lashes look like they already have mascara on them.

Camilla Kirk-Reynolds, an award-winning eyelash extension specialist, says, "A good technician will take into account your whole look and your lifestyle, as well as your face and eye shape. It is even possible to create the appearance of symmetry in the eye shape, face or eyelids, or create lift in eyes where there is none."

One concern is that extensions damage the lashes, but this doesn't have to be the case if you find a skilled technician. They require infills every 3-4 weeks to maintain the appearance, and when you want a break, you let them grow out or have them removed.

Brazilian Blow-Dry

The Brazilian blow-dry is the answer you need to fight frizzy hair caused by the damp British weather. It's a semi-permanent way of smoothing and improving the condition of your hair for up to four months. If you have frizzy hair, not only will your hair become more manageable, but you'll save yourself a lot of time blow-drying or straightening your hair, as when you wash your hair, it is already smooth and straight.

Keratin, a substance that exists naturally in nails, skin and hair, is applied to your hair for about half an hour, and then your hair is blow-dried, so the keratin treatment is locked in. Some treatments also run hot straighteners through your hair to leave it straight and smooth. The treatment can also improve the condition of your hair, as the Keratin forms a protective protein layer that nourishes the hair cuticles.

Clothes Care

Good clothes care is an essential part of your overall polish and grooming. You don't need to buy new items all the time if you invest in good quality clothes and take care of them.

Make sure you check yourself in your full-length mirror from all sides before leaving the house. Double check that the hem of your trousers, coat or dress is intact, and there aren't any stains you hadn't noticed. Make sure the 'X stitch' has been removed from the bottom of the vent at the back of your jacket or coat. If buttons come loose, have them sewn back on as soon as possible. If an item does not fit, is stained or coming undone, have it dealt with as soon as you notice, otherwise, it will remain in the wardrobe unworn, or worse, not give the best impression of you.

> DRESS SHABBILY, THEY NOTICE THE DRESS.
> DRESS IMPECCABLY, THEY NOTICE THE WOMAN
>
> Coco Chanel

Have a lint roller and clothes brush to hand by the mirror, especially if you have a cat or dog. Check that your shoulders are free of dandruff flakes.

Many modern fabrics, such as jersey and silk, are better steamed. This helps to avoid the ironing shine that can occur on some fabrics. I recommend investing in a small, handheld travel steamer. They are perfect for business travel as you can get rid of any creases quickly and easily and are ideal when an item doesn't require the full ironing board treatment.

Bobbly knitwear is not a good look, so a de-bobbler is another item you should not be without. Most knitwear will start to bobble, even expensive cashmere. Removing the bobbles will make a jumper look like new. I prefer to use a battery operated one, but others swear by a traditional cashmere comb.

Shoes need to be checked regularly, polished and re-heeled. You should have more than one pair of any staples that you wear a lot to avoid wearing them every day and running them into the ground. Make sure you use a protector spray on new shoes, especially suede ones. Heels that are scuffed look unprofessional, however expensive they are. Your shoes do not need to look 'out of the box' new, just not tired and over worn. If you do a lot of presenting, or appear in front of groups or on a stage, it is even more important that they are in perfect condition, as you do not want people to be distracted from what you are saying as they ponder your battered shoes.

Leather handbags are big investment pieces that will last you a few years at least, and much longer if they are good quality and treated well. There are specialist handbag care companies who repair damaged and tired looking handbags so they look as good as new.

7.1 YOUR GROOMING ROUTINE

Wherever you sit on a grooming scale, it's worth another look in the mirror, and in your make-up bag, and taking a moment for an honest self-reflection on how you are looking.

Self-awareness is key, so assess where you are at, and do so honestly.

- ARE YOU WEARING TOO MUCH MAKE-UP, OR NOT ENOUGH?

- COULD YOUR MAKE-UP DO WITH AN UPDATE?

- IS YOUR MAKE-UP APPLIED WELL?

- ARE THE MAKE-UP BRANDS YOU USE GOOD QUALITY?

- HAVE YOU HAD A CLEAR OUT OF YOUR MAKE-UP BAG IN THE LAST YEAR TO GET RID OF OUT-OF-DATE PRODUCTS?

- WHAT KIND OF HAIRSTYLES DO YOU LIKE? SEARCH PINTEREST AND SEE WHAT COMES UP, LOOKING FOR STYLES THAT ARE A REALISTIC OPTION FOR YOU, WITH YOUR LIFESTYLE AND TYPE OF HAIR.

- IS IT WORTH CONSIDERING ANY OF THE LONGER-TERM GROOMING OPTIONS DISCUSSED?

- DO YOU OWN A LINT ROLLER, STEAMER, AND DE-BOBBLER? IF NOT, ORDER THEM.

Looking your best is not a one-off event. Your grooming will need to be kept on top of daily and then revisited periodically. Some days will require you to look more polished than others, but the important point is to establish a routine. Have your go-to people and services to help you look your best, as and when you require them, including a hairdresser you know and trust, a couple of places you can get a manicure, and a make-up artist if you attend important events or are regularly speaking or presenting.

> **"**
>
> LEADERS ARE MADE, THEY ARE NOT BORN.
>
> THEY ARE MADE BY HARD EFFORT,
>
> WHICH IS THE PRICE WHICH
>
> ALL OF US MUST PAY
>
> TO ACHIEVE ANY GOAL THAT IS WORTHWHILE.
>
> **VINCE LOMBARDI**
> **"**

Everyone has different lifestyles and careers, but ensuring you look well put together is essential if you want to achieve career success. Becoming a leader in any field brings with it increased visibility, and so there will be occasions when you will benefit from applying make-up, however small an amount, or having a blow-dry. Consider your goals around your career, audit your grooming honestly, and see if there is room for improvement.

STEP 7 RECAP

You should now have:

- ASSESSED YOUR GROOMING ROUTINE, INCLUDING: MAKE-UP, HAIR, TEETH, SKINCARE, NAILS, AND WHETHER ANY LONGER-TERM SOLUTIONS COULD WORK FOR YOU

- MADE SURE THAT YOU HAVE WHAT YOU NEED TO LOOK AFTER YOUR CLOTHES, SHOES AND ACCESSORIES AND MAKE THEM LAST

"

IT'S NOT ABOUT THE DRESS YOU WEAR,

BUT IT'S ABOUT THE LIFE YOU LEAD

IN THE DRESS.

DIANA VREELAND

"

AFTERWORD

Now that I have walked you through my process and you understand how to achieve a business image that shows you at your best, it's time to implement it.

Having read through all the steps, you now have a clear idea of what is involved, so please get your diary out and start planning when you are going to *make* the time. This is an important point. I know you will not *have* the time, so please don't use that as an excuse!

You'll need to consciously make time to go through the activities, just as you would find time to prepare for an important job interview, presentation or speech. If you feel working on your wardrobe is an important, worthwhile exercise, then you *can* make it happen.

This process will require varying degrees of time, effort and investment to figure out what your ideal wardrobe is, pull it together, and get it working for you. Your new look won't be achieved overnight, it will be an ongoing process, but if you prioritise and plan the time in your diary, it will make it manageable and hopefully enjoyable too!

As I have said previously, regularity and consistency is more important than finding a big block of time when you can do it all in one go. Take it step by step, and try to stick to a schedule and then keep the momentum going. Decide on a deadline date when you want to have a new look by, and then work backwards by booking in when you will spend time on a few of the activities or one of the steps until you get there.

Block out a few evenings or a couple of consecutive weekends when you can put aside an hour or two, and arrange a day midweek for shopping, and take time off work if you need to. The dates and sessions will more than likely change, but by putting time aside in your diary, you have set an intention and made a commitment to yourself that is harder to go back on. Ideally, make sure the time between each session is minimal, as it will be much better if you can go from one step to the next without more than a week between.

The ongoing impression you will make is as important as the first impression. You change, and your circumstances, career and lifestyle will also change. As with your a car, garden or anything else that requires regular maintenance, if you are able to invest a little time every so often to take stock of both yourself and your wardrobe, your look will remain fresh and authentic as it grows and changes with you. It also means you won't need to invest another big chunk of time or money, as you will probably have to initially when starting again from scratch.

Even if clothes and style are still of little interest to you, I genuinely believe you can learn to enjoy and have more fun with your wardrobe. Remember, what you put in, you get out. When you put some thought into it and then begin to see and feel the rewards of showing up in life as your best, most authentic self, I believe it will ignite a new interest in what you wear. You can work through this process on your own, but I recommend you get help with at least a couple of the steps. Maybe you know someone who is also interested in changing their wardrobe, who you could work together with. Having a friend around for the wardrobe clear out can be useful and make it more fun, and having another person on hand to give feedback, get sizes and carry bags is helpful when shopping. But a word of caution, you *really* must value their opinion, admire how they dress, and be confident they can advise you and be objective. So, share your preparation and insights and what you want to achieve.

If you are time poor and want results quickly, you should consider hiring a professional image consultant or personal stylist. They can advise you on your colours, help you review your wardrobe, and with personal shopping. However, be careful not to hand over total responsibility for your image. Even if you are working with a professional, I would encourage you to answer the questions that I have asked you in this book so you can work with your stylist collaboratively, with clarity about your goals and style preferences, and get the best out of their expertise.

"

CLOTHES AREN'T GOING TO

CHANGE THE WORLD.

THE WOMEN THAT WEAR THEM WILL.

ANNE KLEIN

"

I feel women are the future – of politics, industry and business – and for women to reach the higher echelons of society, they need to believe in themselves and be confident in their abilities. They no longer need to look and behave like men; they need to look like themselves, feminine if they want to be, authentic, and confident.

Successful leaders have gravitas and executive presence, and the importance of image in this can often be overlooked. I hope you will take on board the suggestions in this book and make what you wear part of your toolkit for career success and overall well-being.

Getting dressed is like anything else; the people who dress well do so because they spend some time thinking about it and working on it, or they have someone taking care of it for them, because it is worth it. Your wardrobe will not get you to the top on its own, but it will support your endeavours.

I hope that I have inspired you to take some time out of your busy life and invest it in yourself, and ultimately, your career. I would love to hear from you about your experiences and successes, so please do get in touch and let me know how you get on. You can email me at book@lizzieedwards.com.

I wish you the best on your leadership journey and career success, whatever that means to you. I'm here rooting for you, and know you can do it!

ENDNOTES

1. Recruiter.com, *In 2018, Professional Women Are Still Judged by Their Appearances,* 2018, https://www.recruiter.com/i/in-2018-professional-women-are-still-judged-by-their-appearances

2. *The Paradox of Choice; Why More Is Less,* Barry Schwartz, 2005

3. *Royal Society for Public Health, Status of Mind Report,* 2017, https://www.rsph.org.uk/uploads/assets/uploaded/62be270a-a55f-4719-ad668c2ec7a74c2a.pdf

4. *Blink: The Power of Thinking Without Thinking,* Malcolm Gladwell, 2006

5. *Unbuttoned: The Interaction Between Provocativeness of Female Work Attire and Occupational Status,* Howlett, N., Pine, K.J., Cahill, N. et al. Sex Roles (2015) 72: 105, 2015, https://doi.org/10.1007/s11199-015-0450-8

6. *Mind What You Wear: The Psychology of Fashion* (Kindle), Professor Karen J. Pine, 2014, http://psycnet.apa.org/record/2014-38364-001

7. Journal of Experimental Social Psychology, Volume 48, Issue 4, July 2012, *Enclothed Cognition,* Hajo Adam, Adam D.Galinsky,2012, https://doi.org/10.1016/j.jesp.2012.02.008

8. Journal of Experimental Psychology: General, 143(6), 2330-2340, *Sartorial Symbols of Social Class Elicit Class-consistent Behavioral and Physiological Responses: A Dyadic Approach.* Kraus, M. W., & Mendes, W. B.,2014, http://dx.doi.org/10.1037/xge0000023

9. *The Life-Changing Magic of Tidying: A simple, effective way to banish clutter forever*, Marie Kondo, 2014

10. Business Insider UK, *Here's The Real Reason Mark Zuckerberg Wears The Same T-Shirt Every Day*, 2014, http://uk.businessinsider.com/mark-zuckerberg-same-t-shirt-2014-11

11. Vanity Fair, *Obama's Way*, 2012, https://www.vanityfair.com/news/2012/10/michael-lewis-profile-barack-obama

12. The New York Times Magazine, *Do You Suffer From Decision Fatigue?*, 2011, https://www.nytimes.com/2011/08/21/magazine/do-you-suffer-from-decision-fatigue.html

13. The Guardian, *Angela Merkel's Jackets: Many colours but just one look*, 2012, https://www.theguardian.com/fashion/shortcuts/2012/oct/09/angela-merkel-jacket-pantone

14. Journal of Fashion Marketing and Management: An International Journal, Vol. 17 Issue: 1, pp.38-48, The *Influence of Clothing on First Impressions: Rapid and positive responses to minor changes in male attire*, Neil Howlett, Karen Pine, Ismail Orakçıoğlu, Ben Fletcher, 2013, https://doi.org/10.1108/13612021311305128

15. Research in Social Stratification and Mobility, Volume 44, pp.113-123, June 2016, *Gender and the Returns to Attractiveness*, Jaclyn S.Wonga, Andrew M.Penner, 2016, https://doi.org/10.1016/j.rssm.2016.04.002

ADDITIONAL
BOOK RESOURCES

For further support and information, including events and online courses, visit www.lizzieedwards.com

- ## BOOK AND COVER ILLUSTRATIONS

  Marta Siwecka

  www.martasiwecka.com

- ## BEAUTY EXPERTS

  ### Permanent Make-up

  El Truchan

  www.perfectdefinition.co.uk

  ### Eyelash Extensions

  Camilla Kirk-Reynolds

  www.camillalashes.com

ACKNOWLEDGEMENTS

I am so grateful for the encouragement and enthusiasm of so many, but I particularly want to extend a huge thank you to the following people:

My amazingly supportive husband John for believing in everything that I do and helping me in so many ways. I couldn't have written this book without your encouragement through the ups and downs that came with creating it. You have been so patient and understanding. I love you x.

My early test readers; my friends Kat Chidiac and Claire Thorogood, my sisters Rebecca Kent and Caroline Matthews, and Sandra Schwarzer and Karen McElhatton. Your honest, constructive feedback and enthusiasm was invaluable. I am so grateful that you took the time to read what I'd written and share your thoughts.

All my clients, past and present, for trusting me to help you by allowing me to give my opinion on what you wear, rummage through your wardrobe and take you shopping. Without you, I would have no business and there would be no book.

Extra special thanks to everyone who kindly agreed to feature as a case study. Some of your names have been changed to give you anonymity, but you know who you are.

My editor Leila Green for being so patient and encouraging. Thank you for all your hard work, help and advice. I honestly don't know what I'd have done without you!

Marta Siweka, who so beautifully illustrated the cover and inside of this book. Thank you for your talent and your patience.

My friends from *Sister Snog*, who really are a unique gang of businesswomen. I feel so happy I know you. Running my business would be less fun and lonely without you. Thank you, in particular, to Caroline Flanagan and Patty Cruz-Fouchard for being *Badasses* and keeping me inspired and accountable every month.

The beauty experts Florrie White (when we first became friends almost 20 years ago, who would have thought that I would be interviewing you for my book one day!), Camilla Kirk-Reynolds and El Truchan.

Daniel Priestley at *Dent*, who planted the seed back in 2011 that it was a good idea to become an author.

My fellow *KPI 18* participants who became authors and led the way. Getting your books written and published inspired me to keep going and proved that getting published was achievable.

Rochelle Dallas who was such a big help. This book project has been a marathon, and you arrived at the right time to help me across the finish line.

Last but not least, thank you to the trailblazing personal

Style and Image Consultants, Brenda Kinsel and Carla Mathis. When I started my styling business, I sought the best in the world to teach me. You so generously shared your expertise and knowledge, and more importantly, showed me that I could create a successful business by doing something I loved, which would also have a positive impact on people. I will be forever grateful I had the opportunity to learn from you.

CAN I ASK A FAVOUR?

Thank you again for spending your most precious resource, your time, on reading this book. I hope you enjoyed it and found it of value, and if so, I would love it if you could leave a review on Amazon.

It only takes a moment, and your review is invaluable in helping others to find this book among all the other options they have to choose from.

If you have found it to be of value, please spread the word among your network and on social media. The more women who can boost their confidence and increase their impact by improving their image, the better!

WHAT NEXT?

Working With Me

You can find out about the online course of this book at www.lizzieedwards.com, and be the first to hear about any events by signing up to my newsletter.

If you don't want to go through my process alone and are interested in working with me, or one of my team, please visit www.lizzieedwards.com for more information about how we work and the packages available.

If you are an organisation or employer looking for ways to support your women by enabling them to be all that they can be, and so improve their chances of success, contact me to find out about my speaking, workshops or one-to-one executive services.

Keep in Touch!

To receive regular tips, news updates on my services or events, subscribe to my newsletter at www.lizzieedwards.com or connect with me on social media @lizzieedwardsuk

ABOUT THE AUTHOR

Lizzie Edwards is a personal stylist, image consultant and founder of a niche women's workwear styling business in London, UK.

Lizzie studied fashion upon leaving school, and spent her early twenties as a fashion model, living in London, Milan and Paris.

Since setting up her styling business in 2005, she has worked with hundreds of clients, both men and women, but decided in 2016 to focus on helping female senior executives to reach their full potential.

She and her small team of stylists offer one-to-one, in-person style packages and group workshops that provide impactful results by improving and upgrading wardrobes fast.

Lizzie also works with organisations who recognise the role that image plays in their employees' career success and are committed to supporting them with their wardrobe to ensure they fulfil their career potential.

To learn more and get further resources, connect with Lizzie here:

www.lizzieedwards.com

LinkedIn /LizzieEdwards

Other Social Media @LizzieEdwardsUK

48728222R00167

Printed in Poland
by Amazon Fulfillment
Poland Sp. z o.o., Wrocław